CRIES OF THE HEART

Bringing God Near
When He Feels So Far

RAVI ZACHARIAS

WORD PUBLISHING
Nashville•London•Vancouver•Melbourne

CRIES OF THE HEART

Library of Congress Cataloging-in-Publication Data

Zacharias, Ravi K.
Cries of the heart : bringing God near when He feels so far / Ravi Zacharias.
p. cm.
Includes bibliographical references.
ISBN 0-8499-1337-3 (hardcover)
1. Pain—Religious aspects—Christianity. 2. Suffering—Religious aspects—Christianity. 3. Apologetics. 4. Christianity—Essence, genius, nature. I. Title.
BT732.7.Z33 1997 97-46004
248.8'6—dc21 CIP

Printed in the United States of America.

8 9 0 1 2 3 4 5 9 BVG 9 8 7 6 5 4 3 2 1

To the memory of my mother,

Isabella,

who heard my cries long before

I gave voice to them.

Contents

Foreword

SOME PEOPLE CAN MAKE THE TOUGHEST TASK APPEAR SIMPLE. A professional golfer can make the golf swing look easy. A skilled tenor leads the audience to believe anyone could hit those notes. The advanced chemist speaks the language of his discipline with the same effort that we recite the alphabet.

Some make it appear so simple. But then we try it ourselves and we know better.

We swing the club or sing the song or read the book and realize this is no easy chore. Personal attempts only increase our admiration for the one who does what we can only dream of doing.

Perhaps that is why I have such high admiration for Ravi Zacharias. What others do with the golf club or operas or chemistry, Ravi does with Christian thought. He presents lucid answers to tough questions and makes the problems look simple.

We know better, however. There is nothing easy about Ravi's God-given assignment. His first challenge is to wrestle with the issues many prefer to avoid. A sample of his daily diet of thought is listed here in this book: questions of suffering, loneliness, despair, and guilt. Ravi toils among these dilemmas.

But his assignment doesn't end there. He not only walks these shadowy forests; he leaves a trail which guides us through it. And guess what. The map is legible! It is understandable. It is easy, even a joy, to read.

A perfect example is the book you now hold. Paging through this manuscript left me amazed and encouraged. Amazed at the skill of the author. And encouraged that the Author of Life would give this generation such a gifted thinker. For three decades Ravi has done throughout the world what he has done on these pages. He has helped us think without thinking for us.

And he does so with much grace. I remember an observation made by our mutual friend and publisher, the late Kip Jordon. Kip listened to numerous college campus dialogues between Ravi and students. As hostile as such events can become, Kip once told me, "I have never seen Ravi treat one person with disrespect. He always listens patiently, then responds in a manner which honors the one who raised the question."

I have no reservation in recommending that you read this book. When it comes to golf, singing, or chemistry, I can't vouch for Ravi Zacharias. But when it comes to wrestling with tough issues of faith and life, I know of no one who does it better.

MAX LUCADO

Acknowledgments

I AM OFTEN ASKED, after delivering a lecture or a sermon, how long it has taken to prepare that particular presentation. I have determined that any answer that logs up the preparation time in hours or days runs the risk of forgetting the years that went behind a thirty-minute talk. Such, I am afraid, is the risk entailed when expressing gratitude to those who have helped me shape this book. Any omission of names, therefore, is with full recognition of the many men and women and their thoughts that, over the years, have inspired me to think deeply on these questions that shape our souls. I am greatly in their debt.

For this manuscript there is principally one other who has labored with love and sacrifice—my wife, Margie. My heartfelt thanks are due her. Both of us have always valued the input of the final editor, Sue Ann Jones, whose encouragement and suggestions have been consistently thoughtful and refining. We are the better for it. The Word Publishing staff has worked with us with grace and professional excellence. Thanks are also due to Danielle DuRant, who worked on the tedious task of procuring permissions.

As always, I express my appreciation to all my colleagues at work and to my children, who sacrificed much to give me the time to work on this manuscript. Our prayer is that as a result of this work many a cry will be met and that God will be blessed to accept this as an offering first to Him.

The final acknowledgment is something I never thought would have to be expressed in this way. But even as this manuscript has gone to press we have been shocked and deeply grieved by the going home of a beloved friend and wise counselor, Kip Jordon, publisher and executive vice president of Word Publishing. His imprint has been on all of my books as he lovingly challenged me to combine the simple with the sublime. His death is a jolting reminder of the cries addressed in this book. But his life, passionately lived, demonstrated the truths that point to the God of all comfort, whose embrace he now enjoys.

Introduction

SOME TIME AGO my wife, Margie, returned from an errand visibly shaken by a heartrending conversation she had experienced. She was about the very simple task of selecting a picture and a frame when a dialogue began with the owner of the shop. When my wife said that she would like a scene with children in it the woman quite casually asked if the people for whom the picture was being purchased had any children of their own.

"No," she replied, "but that is not by their choice."

There was a momentary pause. Suddenly, like a hydrant uncorked, a question burst with unveiled hostility from the other woman's lips: "Have you ever lost a child?"

Margie was somewhat taken aback and immediately sensed that a terrible tragedy probably lurked behind the abrupt question. The conversation had obviously taken an unsettling turn. But even at that she was not prepared for the flood of emotion and anger that was yet to follow from this one who was still a stranger. The sorry tale quickly unfolded as the woman proceeded to speak of the two children she had lost, each loss inflicting a heartache all its own.

"Now," she added, "I am standing by watching my sister as she is about to lose her child."

There was no masking of her bitterness and no hesitancy about where to ascribe the blame for these tragedies. Unable to utter anything that would alleviate the pain of this gaping wound in the woman's heart, my wife began to say, "I am sorry," when she was interrupted with a stern rebuke, "Don't say anything!"

Margie finally managed to be heard just long enough to say in parting, "I'll be praying for you through this difficult time." But even that brought a crisp rejoinder—"Don't bother."

After leaving her, Margie returned to her car and just sat there, weeping out of shock and out of a longing to reach out to this broken life. Even more, ever since that conversation she has carried with her an unshakable mental picture of a woman's face whose every muscle contorted with anger and anguish—at once seeking a touch yet holding back, yearning for consolation but silencing anyone who sought to help, shoving at people in her way to get to God. Strangely, this episode spawned a friendship, and we have had the wonderful privilege of getting close to this woman and of praying with her in our home. We have even felt her embrace of gratitude and have reflected much as she has tried in numerous ways to say, "Thank you."

But through this all she has represented to us a symbol of smothered cries, genuine and well thought through, and of a search for answers that need time before anger is overcome by trust, and anguish gives way to contentment.

These smothered cries and the wordless reality that infuses every life may well be endemic to the human condition—men, women, young people, and even children. Numerous professional voices are now awakening us from the illusion under which men particularly have lived in many cultures, that strength lies in not feeling. What a price has been paid for living with such amputation! Not every cry is ridden by anguish, but every life has its own cry or has heard the cry of another who is struggling with emotions or passions in need of explanation. Not every struggle is vented with such force, but many a life is governed by much inner conflict. And just as some are able to cope more readily with failure, so also are some better able to handle the vicissitudes of life.

The purpose of this book, therefore, is not simply to apply some healing balm to the bitter pain of an unheard cry; rather, it is to face squarely the reality that all of us in our private moments deal with suppressed cries. Years ago *Reader's Digest* printed an article entitled "When We Are Alone We Dance." The main idea was that when we are alone and nobody is watching, we all have some rhythmic expression. We may not succeed in clicking our heels in midair, but that does not keep us from trying. Within that private world, each one of us also wrestles with some heart-consuming battle. For one it may be the inner ache of loneliness; for another it may be the daunting and haunting specter of guilt. For yet another it may be the question, "Why do I not feel God to be near when I have done all that I know to be right?" And for still another it may be the question of all questions—"Who are You, God?"

The reader will immediately recognize the range of our existential struggles. If anything unites our cultures today it is the unanswered questions we face that have a felt reality. The loneliness of an unloved life is the same in Bombay as it is in Barcelona. The life tormented by guilt is the same for a movie icon in Hollywood as it is for a schoolteacher in Havana. How do I choose a life that has pleasure without living a life that is immoral?

These gnawing questions were underscored by a grim and dreadful incident that took place in New York City some years ago, the culmination of a series of almost indescribable events that had befallen a young woman. The story is too heartrending to repeat. Feeling the silent pain of a whole city, a state senator agonized, "How can so much go wrong in one life and nobody be aware of it?" After days of pondering that obvious question, a city councilman gave the only plausible answer. He said, "Life is too busy and complicated for me to hear the cry of every person in my community. As a matter of fact, I struggle to find time to even hear the cries of my own family. If I had to listen to the cry of everyone in New York City, you may as well ask me to listen to the sound of every blade of grass growing and to the heartbeat of every squirrel. The noise would be deafening on the other side of silence." I doubt that he overstated his point. If the cries of the heart in any community were to be cumulatively sounded, the noise would indeed be deafening.

Where, then, can we go?

There is a place where there is an aggregate of human suffering and questioning. That place is the heart of God. The Bible repeatedly portrays for us the anguished, though sometimes silent, cries of those in need, pleading for one who might bring hope. Of all the stories in the Scriptures none so accurately reflects those varied needs as the story of the woman at the well in her conversation with Jesus. Throughout the book I will periodically be referring to this encounter, which is described in the fourth chapter of John's Gospel. The disciples had left Jesus to get a little rest while they went into town to buy some food. When they returned they were astounded to see Him talking to this Samaritan woman, but they were afraid to ask why He would talk to her or to question what had prompted this curious familiarity.

Jesus is at His best in this dialogue. The woman represented all that was oppressed or rejected in that society. She was a woman, not a man. She was a Samaritan burdened with ethnic rejection. She was discarded and broken from five failed marriages. She identified God with a particular location, not having the faintest clue how to reach Him. Was it possible to have any less self-esteem than this woman in her fragmented world?

Jesus began His tender yet determined task to dislodge her from the well-doctored and cosmetically dressed-up theological jargon she threw at Him so that she could voice the real cry of her heart. Almost like peeling off the layers of an onion, He steadily moved her away from her own fears and prejudices, from her own schemes for self-preservation, from her own ploys for hiding her hurts, to the radiant and thrilling source of her greatest fulfillment, Christ Himself. But He did not stop there; He went further. That "further" will draw some of our attention in this book.

In short, He moved her from the abstract to the concrete, from the concrete to the proximate, from the proximate to the personal. She had come to find water for the thirst of her body. He fulfilled a greater thirst, that of her soul.

When the disciples finally managed to break into the conversation, they asked Jesus if He was not hungry enough to want to eat. But Jesus said, "I have food to eat that you know nothing about." By now completely bewildered, they wondered if someone had already fed Him.

They were on a completely different level of hungers and thirsts while He was about His Father's business to share the bread of life and to open the spring of living water so that one need never thirst again.

In this simple narrative converge our own hungers and God's great longing to fulfill those inner hungers and satisfy those deep longings. I recall on one occasion speaking to a man who had come from a country where much blood had been spilled in internal strife, a land where someone's heart was broken every day by some stray bullet or a hate-filled ideological conflict. He told me that even though for years he had found comfort in the knowledge that Christ had borne his sins, it was a new realization years later when he took note that Christ had borne our sorrows, too. That intimacy with God is a knowledge that has bridged what one knows with what one feels. Such knowledge takes what we know and what we feel seriously. It is not a fatalistic posture that says "so be it" and is resigned to accept what flies in the face of reason. When we learn God's profound answers to every sentiment we feel, we find contentment and courage and live a life of hope and confidence. We then make every day count with significance while treasuring His thoughts and harnessing our feelings.

For too long we have forced a dichotomy between fact and feeling and have unwittingly bought into systems of thought that held on to the one while doing disservice to the other. Voltaire once remarked that all of man's miseries are a reflection of his grandeur. In other words, our senses and sensations can and ought to be joint indicators of the eternal and the true. That which God has joined together, let no man put asunder. We well remember the words of the song that ask, "How can it be wrong when it feels so right?" and we might legitimately take issue with that plundering of the objective realm of right and wrong at the mercy of momentary passion.

But there is another side to it: How can things be right when they feel so wrong? That is a much more difficult issue. Does God expect one who is plagued by a lonely existence to dismiss that feeling as unreal? Does the search for a personal God in an impersonal world not raise legitimate questions? Do the questions of a person in agony not count? Must we not have wisdom amidst the myriad pleasures that surround us? That is where this book hopes to lead us. We will not be content to deal with the problems as they surface merely by an intellectual stroke of the pen. We will not stop at the point where the answers are merely stated as glib responses. Our hope will be to bring the whole of our being to engage with the questions and the cries of the heart. Cries are born out of real feelings. So also must joy betoken a real confidence and repose.

There are two comments that must be made regarding the material as it unfolds. First, the particular theme of pain and suffering is as much a philosophical problem as it is an emotional one. As I have dealt with it under the title "The Cry for a Reason in Suffering," I have based my study on the Book of Job. I have resisted the temptation to get too philosophical so as not to break into the train of thought or rob us of the emotional strength of the material. Hence, I have brought the weight of logic to bear upon only a small portion of the subject; the primary thrust of the material is a response to the felt problem of pain when we face it personally. For those who want to wrestle with it philosophically I have, therefore, added a postscript at the end of the book that addresses the thorny issue of how God could even create a world when He knew suffering would come as a result. That is a slightly different question to Job's.

Also, in two of the themes, pleasure and loneliness, there was more that could have been said to complete the answer. However, those thoughts I have included and brought to their legitimate culmination in the final chapter. The reason will be obvious as you come to it.

In the Psalms David described himself as one wounded and crying in his bed at night. This same David spoke of the happiness that came when he took that cry to the Lord. With that same confidence, let us begin our journey to respond to the cries of the heart. We might be surprised to know how much bottled-up sentiment will be uncovered. When God speaks we will not respond by saying, "Don't say a thing." Rather, we will be soothed by His touch and will rest in His comfort, knowing that He has bothered to hear our cries and to come near in our need. We too will long to say to Him, "Thank you."

One

The Cry to Know God

AT A CHRISTMAS EVE SERVICE we attended one year, a short play was featured. It was principally a monologue by Joseph as, moments after the birth of Jesus, he held the little one in his arms and spoke to Him. He looked into the face of the baby and with all the gushings and musings of a new father playfully talked about His resemblance to his mother. But then he paused and in all seriousness whispered, "I wonder what your father looks like . . ." One could sense that the hundreds in the pews echoed those sentiments.

Throughout history artists, writers, musicians, scholars, and all who have read of the life of Jesus have wondered what He looked like. Interestingly enough, those who actually saw Him took the search a step further—"Show us the Father," they said. One of the first questions the would-be disciples asked Him was, "Where do You live?" (Sheer humor would have wanted Him to respond, "You'd never believe Me if I told you!") In the light of His manner and His power, it was a legitimate mystery that prompted them to ask Him for His address. Whether it is the Jesus of history or God the Creator, we have all pondered on His likeness.

Saint Augustine wrote of a Faustian-type encounter he had when a momentary delight was offered to him. The only condition was that he would forfeit the pleasure of ever seeing God. He concluded without a struggle: "No pleasure is worth that loss."

In His grace and wisdom, God has blessed us with intellects and senses that long to see, to hear, and to know Him. At the same time He has given us the wonderful privilege of allowing our imagination to provide both liberty and limitation. He cautioned us never to make a graven image. It bears reminding that though we exalt a man or a woman by carving him or her in stone or painting on canvas, attempting the same for God, we are warned, only reduces Him. Circumscribing God is fraught with the peril of our own prejudice, to say nothing of it being contradictory.

We are also reminded in the Scriptures that no one could "see God" and live. When Moses cried out that he would not cross over into Canaan unless God revealed to him His glory, God answered:

> There is a place near me where you may stand on a rock. When my glory passes by, I will put you in a cleft in the rock and cover you with my hand until I have passed by. Then I will remove my hand and you will see my back; but my face must not be seen. (Exod. 33:21–23)

The Scriptures are scanty with reference to Jesus' physical appearance. We shall all, therefore, have to await the day when "every eye will see him" (Rev. 1:7). Even at that, we cannot help but wonder what "seeing" Him will entail.

But where those physical features have been guardedly presented, and with reason, the Scriptures are profuse in describing for us God's person, His character, and how He has chosen to reveal Himself. In mining the wealth of that content we come to understand how profoundly He has responded to the cry of the human heart—"Who are You, God?" This ought to be the paramount quest of every man, woman, and child, because from that knowledge flows every other answer to the cries of the heart and mind.

Charles Haddon Spurgeon worded it well:

> The proper study of the Christian is the Godhead. The highest science, the loftiest speculation, the mightiest philosophy which can engage the attention of a child of God is the name, the nature, the person, the doings, and the existence of the great God. . . . There is something exceedingly improving to the mind in a contemplation of divinity. It is a subject so vast, that all our tools are lost in its immensity; so deep, that our pride is drowned in its infinity. Other subjects we can comprehend and grapple with; in them we feel a kind of self contentment, and go on our way with the thought, "Behold I am wise." But when we come to this master science, finding that our plumb line cannot sound its depth, and that our eagle eye cannot see its height, we turn away with the thought, I am but of yesterday and know nothing.[1]

God is the central theme of the writers of Scripture. They submerged themselves in the pursuit of the knowledge of Him, and as they were borne by the Holy Spirit, have left for us that revelation. In the very earliest days of God's self-disclosure we are given a glimpse of the fear that overwhelmed the people as they awaited Moses' return from the top of the mountain. They knew their leader stood in a unique position in all creation when he was beckoned by God to come to the mountain to receive His commands. There was interaction with God, there was communion with God, and there was instruction from God. As we begin this study let us put ourselves into the place of one who raised the question of who God is and learn how over time we have found the consummate answer. I am confident that the truths we uncover will stretch the mind and fill the heart.

THE FOXHOLE REALITY

I turn to a classic passage, the prayer of Jehoshaphat in 2 Chronicles 20. A massive army was closing in on his forces, and he called the nation to prayer. It is not surprising that in times of war some of the most impassioned prayers of the heart have been prayed. How they are prayed and by whom they are prayed in itself makes for a fascinating study. History is replete with the prayers of generals on the eve of a great war.

The annals of Russian history tell us of that pivotal turning point when Napoleon had surrounded Moscow and, indeed, its spires were being torched and burned. Knowing he was on the verge of humiliation and defeat, the czar was on his face before God in a church in Saint Petersburg, pleading for God to save his nation.

No, he was not a devout man with a natural bent for prayer. This czar, in fact, had lived a dissolute life. Earlier he had intentionally appointed a vile man as archbishop in the hope of gaining an ally in his own wicked lifestyle. But God works through the schemes and ploys of political demagogues, and after taking office the archbishop no longer wanted to mock God. In a completely surprising move to all, he surrendered his life to Christ.

As the nation tottered on the brink of defeat, the czar himself sought God in repentance and prayer. God answered his plea and sent a minor, minor prophet—the winter. The rest is history.

On February 24, 1986, the history of the Filipino people records the same cry of desperation. Eight hundred soldiers were open targets before President Ferdinand Marcos's air force. Nervously they stood, watching these aircraft hover over them and knowing that their attempt at a peaceful revolution could end in moments with their small army being blown apart. But they were not just standing there; they were being led in Scripture reading and prayer. Sure that the end was near, General Honesto Isleta (who personally told me this story when he was a student in a course I was teaching in the Philippines) was reading to them from Psalm 91:[2]

> He who dwells in the shelter of the Most High
>   will rest in the shadow of the Almighty.
> I will say of the LORD, "He is my refuge and my fortress,
>   my God, in whom I trust." . . .

> He will cover you with his feathers,
> and under his wings you will find refuge;
> his faithfulness will be your shield and rampart. (vv. 1, 2, 4)

Even as they heard the Word of the Lord being read to them, the whirring of the encroaching aircraft overhead grew louder. But something was happening of which they were not aware. As the planes came closer, instead of wiping out this meager handful on the ground, one by one the pilots defected and landed. That story of the "Bloodless Revolution" is now history, too.

In the Persian Gulf War in 1991 General Norman Schwarzkopf was at the helm of the greatest firepower ever brought under the command of one man. He has gone on record saying that even as the Stealth bombers were closing in on their targets to begin the war, he was in prayer.

Such situational prayers do not always have national import, but the principle filters down to each of us. A pastor friend of ours told us of a happening one Sunday afternoon when all was peaceful in his family's home. Suddenly they heard some shouting, arguing, and scuffling in their backyard. Hurrying over to the window, they saw their little boy with fists clenched, staring down a bigger neighborhood kid. Before they could run to their son's rescue, they heard him scream out, in what sounded like a war cry, "I come to you in the name of the Lord Almighty, the God of the armies of Israel!"

The poor neighborhood bully, thoroughly disoriented by this terrifying formula that was foreign to his little heathen mind, turned around and bolted as fast as his feet could take him. My pastor friend said they laughed hilariously, knowing that the application of the Sunday school lesson that morning on David and Goliath was evidently made in their son's afternoon altercation.

From life's bigger and more serious battles to the childhood conflicts we face, we pray in times of confrontation with a bigger enemy. But in Jehoshaphat's instance, it was more than that. There is something profoundly theological in the very content of his prayer. Such prayers are rare and have much to teach us. This was more than just a cry for help or for victory. This was a plea that those who were in the thick of this conflict would know who God was. Jehoshaphat did not just ask for intervention; he sought the very person and the presence of God. Only in that context did he believe he would find victory in his own life before any victory in battle. Jehoshaphat raised three questions in his prayer about God. As we look at those questions, we will spend the majority of our time on the first, because the answers to the other two hinge on it.

As we wade through these ideas, the most important question will be answered: "Who are You, God?" I should warn the reader that the journey through the ideas we will wrestle with will not always be an easy one. Like climbing a mountain, there is no shortcut. But I am certain that if we think this through as we travel together we will reach the top. The patience and labor will be worth it, and the rewards will be proportionate.

The Hazard of Perception

Jehoshaphat's prayer begins in 2 Chronicles 20:6:

> O LORD, God of our fathers, are you not the God who is in heaven? You rule over all the kingdoms of the nations. Power and might are in your hand, and no one can withstand you.

What a way to open his prayer—"Are you not . . . ?" How was he going to complete that? It was meant both as a question and as an affirmation to the people as they feared the future. I would venture to suggest that if one hundred people chosen at random were asked to fill in the blank space after "Are you not . . . ?" the diverse responses would inevitably establish that God seems to be something different to each person. Not only that, but chances are that to most the answer would be in the context of their most immediate fear or need.

The December 1990 issue of *Life* magazine featured an article entitled "Who is God?" The intention was to present the perceptions about

God of a variety of people ranging from scientists to ministers to homemakers. The story each one told was intriguing. An elderly woman dying of cancer spoke of the nearness of God to her in her fatal disease. A minister who had gone astray and now lived with the specter of AIDS spoke of the mercy and forgiveness of God while he was yet in that pitiful condition. A molecular biologist spoke of the marvels of his discipline that pointed him to God the creator and designer. To that point there was a common thread. God was personal, caring, comforting, revealing . . . a friend.

But then a dramatic shift began. God was not so much a person as He was a power. Truth was not an embodiment as much as it was an idea. Salvation was not a condition as much as it was a pursuit. The further along one read the more muddled the concepts became, and an unmistakable reality emerged: The narrower the definition of God became, the smaller the group that would subscribe to it.

The article brought to memory an interview some years ago with Madalyn Murray O'Hair, the outspoken atheist. On a talk show with David Frost the audience was asked how many of them believed in God. The number was overwhelming. Frost looked at O'Hair and presented the challenge that she was clearly against the mainstream of societal beliefs. O'Hair made a disrespectful counterpoint of her audience's inability to think rationally on these issues. Theologian R. C. Sproul has rightly stated that had she thought clearly herself, she could have sealed the point in her favor, with a knockout argument. She could have just said, "How many of you believe that God exists and that His Son, Jesus, was born of a virgin, that He died on the cross, rose again from the dead, and is the only way to God?" A staggering number would have dropped their hands with that question.

As conciliatory as an audience's intentions may be, there is little doubt that their concepts of God would vary and that there would not emerge a monolithic picture of who God is. To one He may be a political ruler who incites people to overthrow any other power that refuses to enforce His revelation. To another He may be the God who works in individual lives rather than in systems. To yet another it is His spirit that unfolds in history. To many He may just be "whatever you want Him to be."

"Who are You, God?" begets contradictory answers when left at the mercy of individual whim. This is not to minimize individual perceptions; it is only to establish that perceptions differ from person to person, and when they are in contradiction to other perceptions there is no point of reference for knowing which perception is correct. With the bewildering array of answers that are offered to this all-important question, the seeker after God turns from experience to see if the philosopher can arbitrate and settle once and for all just who God is.

THE PROBLEM WITH ARGUMENT

Much to a thinking person's disappointment, the waters here get even more muddied, for now the very notion of God's existence is put to the test. One has only to read the numerous debates that have taken place to demonstrate how easy it is for some philosophers to climb the ladder of abstraction, supposedly in an effort to clarify the issues. One such debate pitted two outstanding scholars against each other, J. P. Moreland defending Christian theism and Kai Nielsen, a renowned atheistic philosopher.[3]

J. P. Moreland did a masterful job of presenting the various arguments that speak for an intelligent, personal, first cause of the universe. Nielsen failed to respond to most of Moreland's well-thought-through and graciously presented defense of the Christian faith. Instead, he hung his whole belief system on just one counterargument. "If you asked me who made this pizza, I can show you who made it. When I ask you to show me the God who made this world, you have nobody to show me. There is no denotative proof for this God of yours," he said.

To anyone who has done his or her philosophical homework, this was a weak response to a mountain of evidence. Several other philosophers responded to Professor Nielsen, and one in particular showed the hollowness of presuming that his argument for denotation was sufficient to demolish all other arguments. But Nielsen was convinced that that was all he needed in his arsenal. Thus, the debate continued to go back and forth until it became dubious whether even at its best, argument is able to untangle the mystery of God for the unwilling. Once again, this is not to minimize philosophical debate but only to show both its limitations and the ease with which the sophisticated can hide behind a mountain of words.

Having dabbled in philosophy a fair bit and enjoyed it, I am nevertheless convinced that if one is quite adept in his or her discipline, he or she can almost "prove" anything that one desires. There is no point in arguing with a person who is determined to explain everything away. Nothing good can come if the will is wrong.

As the material in this and other debates that have taken place on this subject is considered, it is impossible not to admire and respect the intellectual strength behind sound arguments. The knowledge and erudition are enviable, even as the motivation for each one involved could be assumed to be genuine. But there is a gnawing discomfort that when the material rises to such high levels, most of us are blocked from the debate. The cry comes from within: Is this really what it would take to establish the plausibility of God in a philosopher's universe? For some it may be effective, but for multitudes all these words tend only to obscure the existential struggle of each one of us.

Undoubtedly such learning serves a great purpose in helping to clear important hurdles for those in the front lines of intellectual combat. But it is still a huge chasm of thought that can be crossed only by a few. Frustration reaches a high point when both experience and argument taken independently have reached their limit. As a result, all kinds of caricatures of God can be fashioned to fit our desires.

In his book *Running with Horses,* Eugene Peterson tells a fascinating story. While he was a theological student he also worked on the pastoral staff of a church in New York City. The caretaker of the church, a man by the name of Willi Ossa, was an artist by day and a janitor at night. He was a German who had grown up during the war years and later married an American girl. Along with their infant child they now made their home in New York. Willi offered to do a portrait of Eugene Peterson, and Peterson agreed, only to keep the friendship and contact going, for there was a very quiet but hostile attitude toward Christianity in Ossa's life. Day after day, week after week, Peterson would set aside the time to sit in front of the artist. Throughout this time Ossa never permitted Peterson to see how he was progressing.

One day, Willi Ossa's wife dropped in while he was painting, and with one look at the picture she shrieked, "Krank! Krank!" (The word was German for "sick.") "You paint him to look like a corpse!" she said.

Ossa, visibly upset by this untimely revelation of his purpose, snapped back, "Nicht krank, aber keine Gnade." ("He's not sick; that is the way he will look when the compassion is gone, when the mercy gets squeezed out of him.")

It did not take long for Peterson to realize what this was all about. Willi Ossa hated the church and thought Christians were hypocritical. He blamed the state church of his homeland for not having done more to stem the atrocities of the Holocaust. Now, somewhat grateful for Peterson's friendship, he wanted him to know what would happen to him if he persisted in the "Christian way." It is a very sad story and an indictment against Christendom's historic baggage.

But behind it all, one wonders if that is not the picture of God that many have. Born out of some aberrant "experience" or distilled from some radical philosophy, they see God as a sharp implacable hostility devoid of love and mercy. Secular philosophers reduce Him to a single idea. Sociologists study Him as a cultural phenomenon. Existentialists squeeze Him into a feeling. Is it any wonder the honest seeker cries out, "Who are You, God?"

This is the danger to which much debate and religion based only upon experience can lead people. We are left with an artist's version of how God looks, conditioned principally by the artist's own prejudice or perception of God.

THE FACT OF REVELATION

With the pitfalls of argument and the distorting capacity of experience, we move to a dramatically different source of who God is, and that is the disclosure of God in the Scriptures. God has revealed Himself to us in very significant passages. We get snapshots from the various writers as they were inspired by His Holy Spirit. Here is that familiar and magnificent section from the prophet Isaiah.

> Do you not know?
>   Have you not heard?
> Has it not been told you from the beginning?
>   Have you not understood since the earth was founded?
> He sits enthroned above the circle of the earth,
>   and its people are like grasshoppers.
> He stretches out the heavens like a canopy,
>   and spreads them out like a tent to live in.
> He brings princes to naught
>   and reduces the rulers of this world to nothing.
> No sooner are they planted,
>   no sooner are they sown,
>   no sooner do they take root in the ground,
> than he blows on them and they wither,
>   and a whirlwind sweeps them away like chaff.
>
> "To whom will you compare me?
>   Or who is my equal?" says the Holy One.
> Lift your eyes and look to the heavens:
>   Who created all these?
> He who brings out the starry host one by one,
>   and calls them each by name.
> Because of his great power and mighty strength,
>   not one of them is missing. . . .

Do you not know?
  Have you not heard?
The LORD is the everlasting God,
  the Creator of the ends of the earth.
He will not grow tired or weary,
  and his understanding no one can fathom.
He gives strength to the weary
  and increases the power of the weak.
Even youths grow tired and weary,
  and young men stumble and fall;
but those who hope in the LORD
  will renew their strength.
They will soar on wings like eagles;
  they will run and not grow weary,
  they will walk and not be faint. (Isa. 40:21–26, 28–31)

Listen to the words of Micah the prophet, whose very name means "Who is like Yahweh?":

Hear, O peoples, all of you,
  listen, O earth and all who are in it,
that the Sovereign LORD may witness against you,
  the Lord from his holy temple.

Look! The LORD is coming from his dwelling place;
  he comes down and treads the high places of the earth.
The mountains melt beneath him
  and the valleys split apart,
like wax before the fire,
  like water rushing down a slope.
All this is because of Jacob's transgression. (Micah 1:2–5)

This is the same Micah who, having talked of the terror that a sinner might feel when he faces judgment, ends with these words:

> Who is a God like you,
> who pardons sin and forgives the transgression . . . ?
> You do not stay angry forever
> but delight to show mercy.
> You will again have compassion on us;
> You will tread our sins underfoot
> and hurl our iniquities into the depths of the sea.
> (Micah 7:18–19)

Consider also the descriptions of the encounters between God and Moses, between the angel and Mary, and between Jesus and Saul of Tarsus. Placed beside the words of the prophets, a picture emerges of men and women struggling to speak in God's presence and then, in the afterglow, finding words insufficient to express what they felt. It is no surprise at all that when we get to Paul's description of a vision in which he was taken into "the third heaven" he says, "Whether in the body or out of the body, I cannot tell." He was speechless—not a common occurrence for Paul. He summed it up with the words:

> No eye has seen,
> no ear has heard,
> no mind has conceived
> what God has prepared for those who love him. (1 Cor. 2:9)

John, who was privileged to receive the final revelation, also found words failing him. His best attempt is the oft-repeated refrain, "Like unto. . . . Like unto." How does one describe that for which all analogies fall short?

THE STRENGTH AND LIMITATION OF THEOLOGY

Of the handful of clear concepts that emerge when these grand truths are summarized, four are principal. The first is that of God's sovereignty. The second is His holiness. The third is His omniscience, and the fourth His immutability. Each of these concepts warrants volumes of exposition. But one little finger of thought is all we can grasp at this point to help us get to the top.

When we read of God's sovereignty, we read of a world that was created out of nothing. We read that God directs the paths of individuals and even of history. We read of His power over the elements. We read of His self-existence, uncaused by any other force or reason. In short, God is the sovereign ruler of the universe.

James Montgomery Boice, editor and contributor to that fine piece of work *Our Sovereign God*, introduces his subject with the story of a family friend of Donald Grey Barnhouse. He was a member of the United States Cavalry at a time when there were very few automobiles or airplanes. This proud soldier was prone to tell story after story of his glorified and exciting life as part of the cavalry. On one occasion he said, "The most important thing in the entire armed forces of the United States is a cavalry general. After that there is a cavalry colonel, a cavalry major, a cavalry captain, a cavalry lieutenant, a cavalry sergeant, and a cavalry trooper. And then there is the cavalry trooper's horse . . . followed by nothing, followed by nothing, followed by a general in the infantry." His point was made. Anything to do with the cavalry was part of everything. Then there was nothing, so that the best of whatever followed was less than nothing, by comparison.

Years later, when Barnhouse was asked what the most important doctrine of God was, he pointed to God's sovereignty. Everything else was under that. The fact is that if God were not sovereign, how on earth did we come to be and where on earth are we headed? If there were no one "in charge" or in control, how frightening this existence would be. God identified Himself as the "I Am." What better way to describe the One who at all times, is. Nothing else and no one else can lay claim to that description. Everything else has been brought into being. For God there is no beginning or end. There never was a time when He was not, and it is impossible for Him not to be. It is the sovereignty of God that gives life and history a purpose. He is sovereign in the best and purest sense of the term.

The second concept that emerges is the holiness of God. Seven out of every twelve references to the name of God in the Old Testament refer to Him as holy. In Him there is nothing that is untrue, destructive, or imperfect. There is an essential purity by which all else gains its definition of good and evil. He cannot lie and will not commit wrong.

In the early part of this century a very significant book was written by the German scholar Rudolf Otto, a work translated into English as *The Idea of the Holy.* Otto made a vital point that although the notion of moral purity is present in the idea of holiness, the concept of holiness far exceeds mere morality. He called it an "extra," a certain "overplus" that goes well beyond goodness, a "tremendous mystery."[4] A. W. Tozer, one of the most creative writers on this theme of God's holiness, makes a similar comment.

> Neither the writer nor the reader of these words is qualified to appreciate the holiness of God. Quite literally a new channel must be cut through the desert of our minds to allow the sweet waters of truth that will heal our great sickness to flow in. We cannot grasp the true meaning of the divine holiness by thinking of someone or something very pure and then raising the concept to the highest degree we are capable of. God's holiness is not simply the best we know infinitely bettered. We know nothing like the divine holiness. It stands apart, unique, unapproachable, incomprehensible and unattainable. The natural man is blind to it. He may fear God's power and admire His wisdom, but His holiness he cannot even imagine.[5]

The holiness of God is a theme that has captured the minds of theologians and songwriters alike, and the more profound the treatment of it the less qualified the writer feels in addressing it.

Not only do the concepts of God's sovereignty and God's holiness emerge, but we notice the equally mysterious attribute of God's omniscience. In very straightforward terms it means that God possesses perfect knowledge and, therefore, has no need to learn. "Who has understood the mind of the LORD, or instructed him as his counselor?" (Isa. 40:13). Here again, A. W. Tozer summarizes its implications so well:

> God knows instantly and effortlessly all matter and all matters, all mind and every mind, all spirit and every spirit and all the spirits, all being and every being, all creaturehood and all creatures, every plurality and all pluralities, all law and every law, all relations, all causes, all thoughts, all mysteries, all enigmas, all feeling, all desires, every unuttered secret, all thrones and dominions, all personalities, all things visible and invisible in heaven and in earth, motion, space, time, life, death, good, evil, heaven and hell.[6]

The fourth attribute is God's immutability. He is indestructible and unchanging. He is not capricious and whimsical but will always act in keeping with His character.

But something very startling surfaces when we attempt to fully understand God's sovereignty, holiness, omniscience, and immutability. If we stop to ponder them, all of these, as wonderful as they are, can throw us into a bit of confusion. Why is that? Here we come up against the limitation of even the queen of disciplines, which is theology.

It is categorically true that while the philosopher's pen may reduce the number of those who can wrestle with the knowledge of God and that belief based on experience alone can result in wrongheaded conclusions about the person of God, the revelation of God in the holy Scriptures gives us the written description by which all other assertions about God must be measured. This is the Word of God. As certain as that is, these very doctrines present an enormous challenge when we reflect upon them.

For instance, the sovereignty of God can seem terribly tyrannical when life suddenly takes a tragic turn. Not everyone voices it, but many have thought it. I recall on one occasion receiving a telephone call from a total stranger who was lying in a hospital bed in a city hundreds of miles away. He had acquired our telephone number through our radio program and insisted that he desperately needed to talk to me. Alerted to his genuine need by the pain in his voice, the call was immediately put through to me. A few days earlier, he had been playing a game of baseball with his colleagues at his office picnic. As he charged toward one of the bases he collided with the man playing that position. So severe was the impact that it snapped his head back. He was calling me from the hospital after receiving word that he would probably be permanently paralyzed from his neck down. Up to that point in his life, he had almost nothing to do with church and with God. But now he was calling those he considered to be "religious people" in search of someone who could heal him.

What a tragedy for a man in his forties, with a young family! To him the concept of God's sovereignty appeared very tyrannical. In a flash, one moment had changed him from complete health with everything to live for to complete paralysis.

The same daunting confusion arises with God's holiness. As human beings we love the concept of holiness when we are in the right, but we are very reticent to apply it when we are wrong. A couple of years ago I read on the front page of a well-known international newspaper the story of a truckdriver in Italy who habitually visited brothels when he was on the road. On one occasion an associate told him about the best brothel he had been to and who he should ask for to receive the best service. He decided to follow up on the recommendation even though it was so close to home. When he arrived at the brothel he asked for the services of that particular prostitute and awaited her arrival. To his utter shock and anger, when the woman walked into the room he discovered she was his wife. He was enraged, realizing that while he had been on the road his wife had been making a living through prostitution. Totally out of control, he grabbed her and would have killed her had he not been restrained.

I could not help shaking my head in utter disbelief as I read this story. Here was a man completely untroubled by his own duplicitous and debauched lifestyle. Yet when the tables were turned on him he could not accept the horror of being a victim of his own philosophy. When two corrupt people expose each other, there is a universal tendency to point the finger. Though we ourselves are decidedly unholy, we invoke a holy standard over someone else. As comforting as it is to hide behind holiness when we bring others to task for their wrongdoings, it becomes a very terrifying concept when we ourselves are brought under the stark scrutiny of its light. What will we do when we stand before a holy God and our wretchedness is disclosed in all its stark horror? Will we blame God?

If sovereignty can seem tyrannical and holiness terrifying, omniscience can seem taunting. David said in the Psalms:

> Where can I go from your Spirit?
>   Where can I flee from your presence?
> If I go up to the heavens, you are there;
>   if I make my bed in the depths, you are there.
> If I rise on the wings of the dawn. . . .
>
> If I say, "Surely the darkness will hide me
>   and the light become night around me,"
> even the darkness will not be dark to you;
>   the night will shine like the day,
>   for darkness is as light to you. (Ps. 139:7–12)

When every thought, every deed, and every intent are known, one can easily begin to feel very threatened and even invaded. Omniscience brings scrutiny to a painful level.

As for God's immutability, we can be certain He will always be sovereign, always be holy, and always be omniscient. Few things intimidate us as human beings as much as the inability to change anything. How torturous this can be when we are so challenged and limited.

THE SUPREME EXPRESSION

In short, these truths come to us at first blush as ideas. As marvelous and glorious as these great doctrines are, there is still an element missing in how best to know Him. That is why God Himself did not stop there. He did something more. Let me get to it by way of an illustration.

When we lived in India a rather novel incident took place with one of our household staff. He hailed from a village, and the city was quite new to him. One day, as a special treat, my mother gave him some money to go and see a movie. This was a first for him. When he returned a couple of hours later, by looking at his face you would have thought he had walked on the surface of the moon. He was ecstatic.

What happened, we asked?

He told us that when he arrived in the theater, the movie had already begun. He walked into the dark hall and stood by the door because he could not see his way around. As it happened he was facing the back of the room from where the movie was being projected, and he saw the beams of light coming through an opening in the wall. He enjoyed that sight for a moment, thinking that this was what a movie was. By chance he turned around and was astounded to see a picture on the screen in splendid color, and in Hindi he let out the equivalent of an Archimedean shout—"Eureka!"

He scrambled over people and stumbled to a seat to sit entranced for the rest of the movie. We had seldom laughed as hard, along with him I might add, thinking at once of his unspoiled demeanor and of his childlike delight.

Somehow, I feel God has done the same with us as He has unfolded to us who He is. Every way in which He spoke to mankind was like that beam bearing the particles of the picture only as a glittering ray—numberless little specks glistening and moving in the same direction—until in one composite, splendor-filled picture, the light fell upon the face of His Son and "We beheld his glory . . . ," said the disciples, "full of grace and truth" (John 1:14 KJV). They shouted, too—"Hosanna! Blessed is he who comes in the name of the Lord!" (John 12:13).

You see, everything a person creates can at best only bear similarity to that person. Like a sculptor who carves his own image or an artist who paints a self-portrait, a person can only bear a similarity to his or her creations. But He who is begotten bears the essence of the one from whom He has been begotten. All of God's creation may show His splendor or beauty up to a point. The Word carried the grand doctrines of His sovereignty, His holiness, His omniscience, and His immutability. But in His crowning expression we see the "only begotten of the Father." He bears the essence of His Father. When they asked of Him, "Show us the Father," He said, "Anyone who has seen me has seen the Father" (John 14:8–9).

For this reason God has reminded us in Hebrews 1:1–2 that:

> In the past God spoke to our forefathers through the prophets at many times and in various ways, but in these last days he has spoken to us by his Son, whom he appointed heir of all things, and through whom he made the universe.

THE CLIMACTIC TRUTH

This ultimate expression is of cardinal importance. It is where the Christian faith departs from all others most significantly. The apostle Paul knew very well the ramifications of this point. He was a man of many cultures: Hebrew by birth, raised and educated in a Greek city, and a citizen of Rome. Each of those cultures had its own ideals. Each had its own metaphor for ultimate reality. Paul was going to show the people of all three cultures that they were looking at the back walls with the beam and they needed to turn and see what the beam pointed to. How did he do this?

The Hebrews gave to the world our moral categories; the Greeks have given us our philosophical categories; the Romans have passed on to us our legal categories.

For the Hebrew the great pursuit of life was symbolized by light: "The LORD is my light and my salvation—whom shall I fear?" (Ps. 27:1). "The people walking in darkness have seen a great light" (Isa. 9:2). "That was the true Light which gives light to every man coming into the world" (John 1:9 NKJV). For the Hebrews light said it all.

For the Greeks, the ultimate goal was knowledge. "You shall know the truth, and the truth shall make you free" (John 8:32 NKJV). "I know whom I have believed . . . ," said the apostle Paul in 2 Timothy 1:12 (NKJV).

For the Romans, the epitome of life was symbolized by glory. Rome was a city to which all roads led. It was not built in a day. It was the eternal city. The glory of the Roman Empire and of the Caesars is proverbial.

Light, knowledge, glory. These were the ideals of the three great cultures. These were the beams of light they stared at. Writing to believers in the city of Corinth that embodied all three influences, the apostle Paul said, "For God, who commanded the light to shine out of darkness, [has] shined in our hearts, to give the *light* of the *knowledge* of the *glory* of God in the face of Jesus Christ" (2 Cor. 4:6 KJV, emphasis added).

What a verse to capture every longing and ideal. And what is more, in this face God's holiness transcended any Hebrew morality, God's omniscience transcended Greece's quest for knowing, and God's sovereignty transcended any Roman glory. All were ultimately shown to us in a face. As if that were not enough, these cultures would someday wither and die, but the unchanging God would always be. Do you want to see God? ask the writers. Look at the face of Christ. In that face every description rises to a perfect level, not just propositional but incarnational.

In this verse we see the culmination of God's revelation. It was not restricted to the philosophy of Greece, nor to the spiritual experience of the Hebrews, nor to the glory of an earthly city. All of those quests were addressed in the absolute truth of the Scriptures. But the ultimate expression of God came to us in a face, "the only begotten of the Father."

Let us take a look at that face, especially as it expressed its heartfelt cry for His disciples, that they might know the full measure of the joy God has to offer (see John 17). We hear the refrain again and again in Jesus' prayer—"Father," "Holy Father," "Father," "Righteous Father," "Father."

Who is God? Let us remember that only that which is begotten bears the essence. And the begotten called Him "Holy Father." Now we, when we are begotten of the Spirit, have His imprint upon us, and we too by His grace and by the redemption of His Son can boldly call Him Father. He is our Holy Father. How unique this is. How precious this is. No other religious faith that I know of calls Him Father.

We have traveled a long way to answer the question, "Who is God?" He is our Holy Father. But what does this mean to us?

Let me explain it as best as I know how. There is a very special family that has blessed our lives. But we would never have known just how special they are if it were not through hearing of a terrible tragedy that occurred in 1989. Greg Simmons was a highly successful businessman. He was full of energy, the best of which was given to Christ and His claim on Greg's life. Greg and his wife, Christie, along with their five children, made their home in Atlanta. He was at the pinnacle of his career, making great inroads into the corporate world with innovative ideas for the insurance industry.

One day Greg took four of his children, aged three to twelve, and a friend to see a recently acquired property in Highlands, North Carolina. They climbed up to a waterfall, and not knowing that there was no support under him, Greg took a fatal step too close to the edge and plummeted a quarter of a mile to his death.

How can one fully comprehend the immediate horror of something like this? We can only plead for the arms of God to hold the loved ones through such a heart-wrenching experience. But out of this grievous event something extraordinary emerged.

Greg's young twelve-year-old son, McKittrick, penned these incredible lines to one of the family's closest friends:

> Dear Mrs. Wieland,
>
> You don't know how much your family helped produce my father. He admired your husband and you alot. He would talk about how good your faith was with God. He tried to be as generous as you all have been to the church and the many other things. Since his death the true friends were revealed. Your family was at the top of the list. You are a great source of energy for my mother

and I. My father loved you very much, and was always trying to be like you. My father was like the three men in the Bible who were given the talents by Jesus. One went out and invested them and multiplied them. One took some stock that failed and came out with nothing. The last one buried them and did nothing with them. All three returned in a few days later and the Lord was pleased with the two who tried to multiply them, but even though the one man had come back with the same amount the Lord was disappointed because he didn't try. My father multiplied and lost many things, but he always was pleasing to the Lord. He got alot of that from your family. My dad was a risk taker and that was just how he was. Genesis 1:1, In the beginning there was God. . . . is what he is really saying. In the beginning of my dad's life he was something special and a risk taker. That was why he was so brilliant and successful.

No one will understand how or why my dad fell into the waterfall. Do yourself a favor and don't try to figure it out. My dad died for his children. He was making sure it was safe for us to come up. You may hear different things but only six saw it and only three understand what really happened. I am one of those. My mom lost her treasure-chest—her husband. Most of the others lost Greg. You lost a best friend. My grandparents lost their son. Forrest, John and Barbra lost their brother. But it is different for me. Totally different for me. He was my best friend and my idol, but when I got my last glimpse of him falling down the falls, I lost my most prized man on earth. He was my father, he was my one and only dad. I had a dream three nights ago but it wasn't a dream. My father is alright. He told me himself. Thank you for being a true friend. I love you alot.

Gregory M. Simmons[7]

It is not possible to read this letter without tears. McKittrick, who usually goes by his middle name, in this instance signed his letter with his first name, for it is the same name as his dad's. "He was my one and only dad," he wrote. This world becomes a very lonely place when sons grow up without their fathers. How much more desolate an existence this would be if the world itself were fatherless.

Who is God? He is our Holy Father. It was William Blake who wrote:

> Tyger! Tyger! burning bright
> In the forests of the night,
> What immortal hand or eye
> Could frame thy fearful symmetry?[8]

There is a fearful symmetry to life. Just as in the darkest night of the soul the brightest light can shine, so also there is a fearful symmetry in juxtaposing "Holy" with "Father."

When God is our Holy Father, sovereignty, holiness, omniscience, and immutability do not terrify us; they leave us full of awe and gratitude. Sovereignty is only tyrannical if it is unbounded by goodness; holiness is only terrifying if it is untempered by grace; omniscience is only taunting if it is unaccompanied by mercy; and immutability is only torturous if there is no guarantee of goodwill. That which God has joined together, let no man put asunder. Thanks be to God, we know with a surety that His grace and goodness and hope and His love underlie all of these attributes. How do we know? Follow the face of Christ to the cross, and you will see it.

We go back, then, to the opening line of Jehoshaphat's prayer, which asked, "Are you not the God who is in heaven?" The next time we read about the God who is in heaven whose name is hallowed, let us remember that He is our Holy Father.

A Needed Memory

The second question Jehoshaphat raised in his prayer was, "Did you not . . . ?" (2 Chron. 20:7). He listed the many crises God had brought them through. He looked back and knew that they would never have reached their present position if it were not for the hand of God upon their lives and upon their nation. On numerous occasions in both the Old and the New Testaments we see how God led them, one step at a time. Early in the Book of Deuteronomy God Himself reminded them of His faithfulness during their forty years of wandering in the wilderness. In his farewell address to the nation in chapter 23, Joshua recounted again God's unfailing love to them. In one of the classic passages of the Old Testament, Nehemiah chapter 9 describes the dedication of the newly rebuilt wall of the city of Jerusalem. The protracted reminder to the people of God's leading and sustaining power over the years of captivity, bringing them to this point in their nation's history, is recorded here for our benefit. In the New Testament the definitive passage is in Acts chapter 7, where Stephen once more reminded the crowd of all that God had done for them, from the call of Abraham all the way to the cross.

This pause to remember is indispensable in our sacred memory. Only as we remember and remind ourselves of God's faithfulness can we even see the pattern God has woven in our lives and learn confidence in His working. That is why, on repeated occasions, God tells the people to place a stone or a marker to remind them to tell the next generation of what God had done.

The August 1988 issue of *Reader's Digest* relates the story of a young twelve-year-old boy living outside Naples, Florida. One afternoon he was playing in the woods along with his dog when suddenly, a searing jolt of furious heat savaged his lower leg. He looked down and saw the massive head of the eastern diamondback rattlesnake that had attacked him even through his shoe. Some time later his father found him lying unconscious in the kitchen of their home. Recognizing what had happened, he put the boy into the car and rushed him several miles to the nearest clinic. On the way his car broke down, and the father stood on the highway pleading for motorists to stop.

Finally, a Haitian farm worker in his pickup pulled onto the shoulder. But the poison had been in the boy for so long by then and the amount of venom was so great that the doctor at the clinic said he could not help him. The only hope was to take him to a hospital, but even at that, he was probably too far gone. The hospital was also a fair distance away. Somehow the boy was still alive when they got him there, only to be told by that team of doctors that he had no chance of survival.

Several days later, to the surprise of everyone, the boy opened his eyes. But a greater surprise was yet to come. The doctor told him that he was a very fortunate young man, for never had he seen anyone survive with so much venom in him for so long.

The young lad shook his head and said that he had known all along that all would be well. He told them that as he was bitten by the snake he had tried to break free but could not. It was the barking of the dog that finally got the snake away.

"I tried to make it back to my home," he continued, "but I started to fall, when a person in white stood by me and picked me up. He carried me into the house and told me that I was going to be sick for some time but that I was not to worry. He would take care of me, and I would be completely well again."

The doctor and the family were speechless. The father tried to dissuade him from his story because "we are not religious people," he said. "We do not go to church." But no matter how hard they tried, the young lad shook his head, telling them he knew exactly what had happened. The article ended by saying that no matter what anyone said to persuade him to change his story, "There is one young boy growing up in America who believes he was carried in the arms of God."

It will be vital for this young man to remember this experience through life's twists and turns. Most of us will not experience a miracle as dramatic as this, but the intervention of God in our lives is equally convincing. That is why the invitation to come to Christ is so significant. When that step is taken, it is important to mark the time and place when the commitment was made. For some the specifics may not always be as easy to anchor in a moment, but the reality of a submission to Christ must always be clear in the memory. That is when we can say, "Did you not . . . ?"

It was with a sad feeling that we visited Saint Petersburg some years ago. We stood by a former church building, now called the Museum of Science and Atheism. This was the very place I referred to in the introduction of this book, where 176 years earlier the Russian czar had fallen on his face before God, pleading for the salvation of his nation. But it had become a monument to atheism. Such are the vagaries of the human mind.

A Confident Hope

This brings us to Jehoshaphat's final question: "Will you not judge them? For we have no power to face this vast army that is attacking us. We do not know what to do, but our eyes are upon you" (2 Chron. 20:12).

Then the chronicler adds this verse. "All the men of Judah, with their wives and children and little ones, stood there before the LORD." The prayer had begun with Jehoshaphat standing before God, and we are told as a postscript that thousands of families, from near and far, stood with him at this trying moment in their history when they thought the battle was beyond their capacity.

What did God give them as an answer? He said, "Do not be afraid or discouraged because of this vast army. For the battle is not yours, but God's" (v. 15). This verse is the middle verse of the Old Testament and rightly so, for it gives the assurance that when we trust in God He will fight for us. The battle is not ours; it is His.

The application of a prayer such as this is crucial. Are You not? . . . Did You not? . . . Will You not? First and foremost it is a reminder to us that God is the One who is and was and will be—the eternal I Am. He never changes. We come to Him as children come into the arms of a loving parent.

Second, it reminds us that God is also the Lord over history. Every time we set our eyes on the size of the battle we will shrink from the task. Every time we look to Him, we leave in peace with the assurance that the battle is the Lord's. It is so easy to be discouraged with the failures and duplicities of politicians and power mongers around the world. We see millions still living under tyrannies and despotisms nicely dressed up in ideological reasons. We witness incredibly harsh rhetoric against things sacred. We are troubled by trends in the arts and particularly by the way television has trivialized the sacred and glorified the profane. Our heroes are more possessed by fame and adulation than they are with the things that matter. Nations that once realized that God is God and is worthy of our worship now treat religion as a vestige of primitive thinking. It seems that a mighty army is closing in upon the church. Is God still in control? He who is and was, will ever be the sovereign Lord of the universe.

Over the years, each time I have seen new attacks upon the name of Christ, I have drawn much comfort from an essay by the noted English writer F. W. Boreham. It is very beautifully titled "The Candle and the Bird."[9] Boreham makes the comment that God's presence is more analogous to a bird than it is to a candle. When a candle is extinguished, the light goes out. But when a bird is driven away, it only leaves to sing its song on another bough.

With that metaphor in mind Boreham traces the mighty moving of God throughout history. Consider, for example, the impact of the Puritans on their world. As it was waning, Milton bemoaned an England that desperately needed the heart of revival once again. Had the light been extinguished? No, only eight years after the untimely death of Joseph Addison, the highly regarded English Christian statesman, a handful of young people were gathered in prayer at Herrnhut, Germany, on the morning of August 13, 1727. Led by twenty-seven-year-old Count Zinzendorf, something of enormous import happened. All the people could remember was that they scarcely knew whether they still belonged to the earth or had actually gone to heaven. This was the birth of the Moravian movement. So even as England was becoming barren of a godly influence, the Moravians were raised up in Germany.

From that movement missionaries were sent to the ends of the globe. But then the Moravian movement began to wane. Had the light been extinguished? No, the bird was singing on a different bough. Later in that century it was William Carey who set foot in India on the very day that the cross was being burned in France. While Voltaire and hostile philosophers had done their work and Europe was threatening slaughter against the gospel, William Carey, with a Bible in one hand and the annals of Moravian Missions in the other, was going to touch the heart of India.

In the dying moments of the Moravian movement, the heart of Wesley was ignited. But again as the Wesleyan revivals were dying out, had the light been extinguished? No, the bird was singing on a different bough. Inspired by the Puritan thinker Chalmers, such leaders as W. C. Burns, Alexander Duff, Robert Murray McCheyne, and Andrew and Horatius Bonar were rising to do a work for God in Scotland. And as Scotland saw its heroes fade, suddenly the voice of Charles Haddon Spurgeon rang out from London to thousands at home and abroad.

No, the light is never extinguished. As a bird, it has sung its song from different boughs. I am convinced that as dark as it may seem to us, there are strains of a melody beginning. The Lord of history may well be tuning His instruments as never before. Let us not look at the dark side.

> . . . while the tired waves, vainly breaking,
>   Seem here no painful inch to gain,
> Far back, through creeks and inlets making,
>   Comes silent, flooding in, the main.
>
> And not by eastern windows only,
>   When daylight comes, comes in the light,
>   In front, the sun climbs slow, how slowly,
> But westward, look, the land is bright![10]

The bird is singing its song. But the melody must first be sung in each of our hearts. The philosopher may debate. The skeptic may scoff. Experience may be deceptive. But the Word of God abides forever, and that Word has shone upon the face of our Lord Jesus Christ. There is the need for constant vigilance, for the tides of history will turn, and any time we think we can change the course by compromise we fail not only our Lord but ourselves. Jehoshaphat's prayer was as much a reminder to him as it was a prayer to God, that He hears us in our need and is in control of history. We can rest in the confidence that the battle is not ours but belongs to God, our Holy Father, who was, who is, and who will be.[10]

Who are You, God? You are sovereign, holy, omniscient, and immutable. You are our Holy Father who is the same yesterday, today, and forever, and our hearts are restless until they find their rest in Thee.

Two

The Cry to Feel My Faith

DANIEL GOLEMAN'S fascinating and best-selling book *Emotional Intelligence* begins with a story that warms and saddens the heart at the same time. It is the story of the last moments of Gary and Mary Jean Chauncey, battling the swirling waters of the river into which the Amtrak train in which they were traveling had plummeted. With every residue of energy they had, both fought desperately to save the life of their eleven-year-old daughter, Andrea. Andrea had cerebral palsy and was bound to a wheelchair. Somehow they managed to push her out into the outstretched arms of the rescuers, but sadly, they themselves perished.[1]

I must confess that I was incredulous at the author's stab at explaining such heroism on the part of Andrea's parents—that we humans behave this way by virtue of evolutionary design for the survival of our progeny. (One is hard-pressed not to ask, If only the reproductive and preserving instincts lay behind the act, why did the healthier preserve the weaker and not themselves?) But I shall resist, because even Goleman was unable to escape the irrationality of just dismissing this act in Darwinistic terms. He went on to add that "only love" could explain such an effort at the cost of losing one's own life. The rest of the book, as the title connotes, wrestles with the subject of human emotions, powerfully demonstrating that the emotional quotient in each one of us may be a truer indicator of our intelligence than the commonly assumed intellectual component. There is in our emotions a storehouse of reasons behind our impulsive responses.

"Don't jump into commitments," we say, because we know how susceptible we are to momentary blindness, based on immediate reactions. Or we say things like, "Sleep on it before you say anything." Once more the implication is that if thought is brought to bear on the present feeling we might do or say something different. We have all found it to be true. And if our feelings regarding our physical well-being are so important to reckon with, how much more important it is that those same feelings be informed when struggling with the nearness or remoteness of God. Feelings on such a matter become life-defining. The imperative is obvious. We must know what is real so that we might base our feelings on what is true.

I was once on a radio program dealing with a completely different subject when, toward the end of the program, a woman called in to say, "I have tried everything, but I do not feel God."

Some days later I received a letter from a young woman who said she had been in her car listening to the program as the questioner raised this great struggle in her heart. "I was so eager to hear your answer to it," she said, "that I pulled over to the side of the road, hoping desperately to hear something that would help me also." Her letter ended on the sad note of her disappointment in such a hope. In just a few lines she summarized the complexity of the problem and her naiveté that in a two- or three-minute answer we could have dealt with an issue as perplexing as this.

AN OLD PROBLEM WITH NEW TWISTS

This yearning to understand what feelings are, why we long to bring support to what we feel, and why we feel what we do has occupied volumes of paper and hours of contemplation. In a strange way it has been the theme of satire, tragedy, and comedy. In a very recent commercial a salesperson was playing the psychologist's role and asking his couch-occupying "patient" to free-associate on the loss of his favorite beverage. With each sentence that underscored the deep sense of loss this poor victim felt, the therapist countered with, "And how did you *feel* about that?"

The humor is intended to exploit the preoccupation with feelings in some forms of therapy, but the irony cannot be missed. We cannot ignore our feelings. From one extreme of a beverage commercial to the other extreme of technological genius, the question of human feelings and the difference they make has surfaced in journals of psychology and more recently even in science and technology.

The technological connection was prompted by the victory of the 1.4-ton IBM computer Deep Blue over the world champion chess player, Gary Kasparov. It is fascinating, though, to note that the best analysts of our time are now trying to underscore what the difference really is between a computer and a human being. Thus far I have read not one that has been able to escape the use of the word *feeling* or *soul* or *God.* All of these words seem impossible to ignore because this is what makes up the heart and essence of human aspiration. Take note, for example, of the words of David Gelertner, professor of computer science at Yale, commenting on Deep Blue's victory. Notice particularly the constant reference to emotions and feelings that are so distinctively human.

> The idea that Deep Blue has a mind is absurd. How can an object that wants nothing, fears nothing, enjoys nothing, needs nothing and cares about nothing have a mind? It can win at chess, but not because it wants to. It isn't happy when it wins or sad when it loses. What are its apres-match plans if it beats Kasparov? Is it hoping to take Deep Pink out for a night on the town? It doesn't care about chess or anything else. It plays the game for the same reason a calculator adds or a toaster toasts: because it is a machine designed for that purpose. . . .

> No matter what amazing feats they perform, inside they will always be the same absolute zero. . . . No computer can achieve artificial thought without achieving artificial emotion too.

Having said that, he ended his article with these words:

> In the long run I doubt if there is any kind of human behavior computers can't fake, any kind of performance they can't put on. It is conceivable that one day computers will be better than humans at nearly everything. I can imagine that a person might someday have a computer for a best friend. That will be sad—like having a dog for your best friend but even sadder. . . . [But] the gap between the human and the surrogate is permanent and will never be closed. Machines will continue to make life easier, healthier, richer and more puzzling. And human beings will continue to care, ultimately, about the same things they always have: about themselves, about one another and, many of them, about God.[2]

What a unique capacity God has put within us—the capacity to feel. Which of us would want to trade away that privilege? Yet at the same time those very feelings leave us desolated in some of life's most difficult experiences. How best to harness this unique endowment and protect that gift from being abused is one of the cries of our hearts. For all of our capacities to feel indicate something beyond the feeling. Author Scott Peck gives us some valuable insights into how the body reacts when it is injured, and in this discussion I borrow from his analogy to demonstrate that such indicators are there for our emotions, too.

When any part of the body is wounded or cut by a sharp instrument, the body responds immediately and in several ways. There is first a dilatation of the small blood vessels, or capillaries, in the vicinity of the injury or infection. This dilatation, which comes from an increased blood flow, is what causes the area to become red, or "inflamed." That enlargement of the vessels also increases porosity in order to allow the white blood cells to escape through the pores and go on a search-and-destroy mission. They literally gobble up the dead cells, the debris, and the bacteria and then return to the blood vessels after having done their job.

But that is not all the dilatation facilitates. The entire swelling makes the nerve endings more sensitive, which brings a tenderness to the area that warns you to protect it from further aggravation or injury. All this feeling engendered in the body is for its well-being and health.

Has not God done a magnificent work in the human body to keep us healthy? Would He do any less with our emotional makeup by not giving us warning signs and healing abilities for our emotions as well? We need to be thankful to God for the protection and sensitivity He has built into us to preserve and to heal so that we may feel what is good and what is destructive.

With that analogy as a starting point, let us look to what our feelings tell us about reality and what reality tells us about our feelings. In a very dramatic sense our privilege to feel and our responsibility toward feeling are indicators about who we are as people and who we are as individuals.

An Outward Look

We will take two steps before we get to God's answers on this important theme. These steps are indispensable as a precursor to finding His help on the felt struggles of the human heart.

We begin first by taking an outward look and recognizing that as different as we are, one from the other, there are some shared feelings expressed quite universally. On a trip some time ago, I was at the airport waiting to catch a plane. The television news monitors seemed to be the point of focus at every departure gate. When I sat down, I wondered what story was gaining such undivided attention. The Timothy McVeigh trial was on, recounting the horrific scene after the bombing of the Alfred P. Murrah Federal Building in Oklahoma City, a crime with which McVeigh was charged and later convicted. His friend was on the witness stand answering questions posed by the prosecutor, and this is what held so many in rapt attention.

"What did he say when you said that even innocent children would die in this planned explosion of the building?" the prosecutor asked.

Every viewer waited with baited breath for the answer. The reply was to the effect that McVeigh had stated that the children were not innocent. "Everyone there is guilty by association with this evil government, and they are getting what they deserve."

At this moment it was impossible to miss the reaction. Every man and woman seated there was shaking his or her head in disbelief. What prompted that all-inclusive reaction? Was it not the silent expression of incredulity that a man could have no twinge of conscience when orchestrating such horror even toward innocent children? Was he a man or a machine? How could he be considered human with such a lack of feeling? Such must have been the unspoken dismay.

More recently, when eighteen-year-old Melissa Drexler excused herself from the middle of a dance at her school prom, alledgedly no one knew what she was about to do. She returned a few minutes later and asked the band to play a song she loved. Nobody in that hall was aware that she had gone to the bathroom, delivered her baby, and alledgedly put the baby in a plastic bag in the garbage, suffocating it to death. It is truly a very sad story. Psychiatrists are describing her as a woman who has amputated her feelings from reality. As far as she is concerned, they say, she discharged a foreign object from her body, and that was all there was to it. Society at large was dumbfounded by the horror of that unconscionable act.

Following that incident the featured article in *People* magazine was the spate of vicious crimes at the hands of the very young. The question raised on the cover asked what has gone wrong with the conscience of a person when so much that is so malevolent is done without emotion?

But it is not only the bizarre that homogenizes our feelings. We watch with widespread approval when we see tears shed in the pursuit of something noble. Kerri Strug, who, with only one foot to bear the weight of her painful landing, courageously vaulted in the 1996 Olympics for the honor and goal of helping her team win a medal for her country, won the emotional applause of a watching world. The tears were hard to restrain. In short, when we take an outward look at the world, our emotions are a vital part of how God has made us.

An Inward Look

Having taken a look at the world of feeling around us we now take a glance at the world of feeling within us. The Socratic maxim—"Know thyself"—is good counsel. On numerous occasions Jesus asked someone with whom He was interacting to look inward and search out the reason for his or her feelings. When Jonah was outraged because the people of Nineveh had repented, God asked him, "Do you have a right to be angry?" There was obviously something within Jonah that prompted his outburst before God. And when Jonah did not answer God the first time, God repeated His question, "Do you have a right to be angry?"

When the prodigal son returned to his father's house, the older brother was agitated at the lavish celebration his father ordered. The father questioned his hard, clearly jealous feelings when the occasion merited this very festivity. And many are familiar with the classic passage of 1 Kings 19, which describes the lowest moment in Elijah's life. He was emotionally depleted from the long battle of words between himself and Jezebel. God came to Elijah in his discouragement, and God said to him, "What are you doing here?" In our jargon we would say, "What has brought you to this point?" Or as the Irish so colloquially and rightfully say, "Is that yourself?"

Being honest with ourselves in an attempt to explain our own sense of God's nearness or distance is critical. Let me present just four questions that will help immensely in better understanding ourselves.

First, it is important to ask ourselves what emotional trappings we have brought into our relationship with God. Was there a problem with unjustifiable anger before we knew Him? Was there a battle with fear that stalked our lives? Did the spirit of negativism and criticism dominate us prior to that moment of commitment to Him? Was there an impulsive and impatient attitude we lived with, wanting everything at the moment we wanted it? Were we very hard on ourselves and riddled with guilt if faced with failure? Was there a moodiness to our disposition?

One of the great songwriters of all time, William Cowper, was just such a person, given to swings of emotion. The author of "God Moves in a Mysterious Way," he is the same man who wrote:

Where is the blessedness I knew
When first I saw the Lord?
Where is the soul-refreshing view
Of Jesus and his word?

What peaceful hours I once enjoyed!
How sweet their memory still!
But they have left an aching void,
The world can never fill.[3]

The Danish philosopher Sören Kierkegaard was mired much of his life in a depressive state. The prophet Elijah was known for his volatility. There was no surprise, therefore, that when he got caught in this conflict with wicked Jezebel he would become depressed to the point of wishing for death.

No one in the New Testament better exemplifies the roller-coaster personality than does the apostle Peter. From challenging Jesus' announcement that the cruelty of the cross awaited Him to cutting off the ear of the high priest's servant, Peter was tossed by the waves of emotion. His daring step into the water at the beckoning of his Master and his panic-stricken cry when he became aware of the size of the waves serve as fitting descriptions of his temperament. It was not out of character that he was the first to deny his Lord and yet the first to run to the tomb when the women came with the message that Jesus had arisen.

How important it is to understand the makeup each one of us possesses, because often we carry the same weaknesses into our relationship with God and wonder why our temperament has not changed. We correctly respond by asking, Did not Christ promise to make all things new? Indeed, God has promised to change us into new beings, but we have often failed to deal with how that comes about. We will do just that before we end this study, but we must recognize that our temperament is a vital component that we must take into consideration. For now, it is important to state that there is a difference between momentary failings and a lifestyle steeped in such weaknesses.

Second, we must ask what prejudices and insecurities we have brought into our relationship with Christ. The disciples proved this very conflict within themselves. They had a great argument over who among them was going to be the greatest in the kingdom. I know of an Olympic athlete who had dreamed of winning the gold medal. Little did he realize the dream was within reach. Yet he told me that literally seconds before the gun was sounded for the finals, "A thought out of nowhere came into my mind. I wondered if my father was watching, because years before he told me that my life would amount to nothing." Evidently the thought was not from nowhere. It came from the scar of a wounded spirit. How deep are the marks we carry with us through life.

Much anguish is spent at the altar of self-acceptance when we have felt such rejection or when we compare ourselves against others. Many bring such insecurities into a relationship with God and do not know how to break their hold. Untold grief paralyzes many of us because we fail to see the differences with which God has made us. We allow ourselves to become irritated by someone else's constant exuberance and wish to deny them that distinctive when, in fact, God has shaped each one of us with a different personality. Conversely, I am just as troubled by the person who, ever riding the crest of an emotional high, fails to recognize the more reserved disposition of someone else. One of the most liberating moments in life is when we are able to accept ourselves as God has made us and are freed from the shackles of trying to be someone we are not and were never meant to be. We then soar to be the unique personality God has given to each of us.

Third, we must ask what indisciplines (the absence or lack of discipline) we brought into our relationship with God. This is often at the heart of much that leaves us restless and uncertain, because in a subtle way the distance we feel is not so much that God is so far away as much as it is that we are so far from where we could be. Indiscipline breeds surrender to the lesser and defeat in the face of opportunity. One of the most painful realities I have found in traveling around the globe is the epidemic proportions of indiscipline. Whether it is in our studies or in our habits, we seem to always find the line of least resistance and then blame God when we fail in our commitment to come to Him on His terms. If we lack the discipline to study, how can we expect to succeed behind the pulpit? If we lack the wisdom to spend wisely, why are we surprised at constant financial hardship? If we lack the commitment to train our children in common courtesies, why are we surprised to find them so rude and insolent? If we fail in the exercise of trust through hard times, why do we expect the rewards of faith?

Goleman tells us of a test given in the 1960s to four-year-olds at a preschool on the Stanford University campus, involving primarily the children of faculty members. The children were given a marshmallow but told not to eat it for fifteen or twenty minutes. As a reward, they would be given another one if they waited. They were then watched, unaware. Some pounded their heads to muster resistance. Others did everything possible to distract themselves. Some just gobbled it up and did not give it a moment's thought. Some patiently waited. Thirty years later the same children were studied, now as adults. The incredible results show a dramatic difference in the ones who had the discipline to wait and the ones who just had no will power. The difference has surfaced in virtually every area of their lives and their performance.[4]

Finally, and possibly of greatest importance in self-searching, we must ask what wrong ideas about God we have brought into our relationship with Him. Jonah believed that God ought to totally destroy the pagans who had lived so violently, but when the Ninevites repented he knew that God's mercy would prevail. Jonah wished God would be other than who He was and that He would judge the people the way Jonah would have judged them.

Os Guinness has a sober warning to those who come to God with their emotions running high but their knowledge running low:

> Mistaken teaching spawns a view of faith that is unbiblical, weak, and ineffective in combating doubts that come from an emotional source. The battle is lost before it begins. The understanding was not in control in time of faith, so it is not in control in time of doubt. The emotions were everything when faith was there, and now that doubt is there they are still everything. All that is different is that they have changed sides. But if emotions are really all that matters, then neither faith nor doubt have anything to do with truth; they are simply the names that we give to their changing moods.[5]

Guinness has clearly touched the raw nerve of feeling and brings, I believe, the most soothing comfort. Once we understand that feelings are vital but not foundational then we delight in the eternality of God's truth and can endure the temporariness of felt distance. But if we reverse that sequence, making our feelings foundational, then closeness and farness are merely descriptive of our moods and may be saying absolutely nothing about the world of fact.

This is subjectivism gone wrong. It is here that I think our illustrations have perhaps fallen short over the years as we have tried in vain to comprehend the mystery of human personality. In the past we have thought of life as a train, the engine of reason pulling the compartment of feeling. I somehow see this as not quite fitting reality. All analogies fail, but some may catch the essence a little better. I see feelings more as a person walking alongside you, always held in the clasp of your knowledge. If that person reverses the grip and your knowledge is clasped by the person of feeling, trouble begins. I do not believe this analogy is far off from what God wants us to understand, and now I shall sustain that, even as we seek His answers.

BRIDGING THE GAP

We have so far established that feelings are not unique to us as individuals. There is common ground we share with one another. But at the same time each one of us brings a different personality into his or her walk with Christ. How may we blend knowledge of the truth with a proportionate feeling so that we will lead our emotions rather than being guided by them? Let me illustrate this, with profound gratitude to God, in an experience our family went through and from which we all learned a lesson that we hope we will never forget. Through this experience I would like to form a bridge to help us cross this chasm between our own frailties and the peace of God that passes all understanding.

Three years ago, our telephone rang at about one-thirty in the morning. It was my sister-in-law, Barbara, calling, filled with fear and dread that something had happened to her husband. He was a flight instructor and was on a trip through the Colorado mountains with two students, training them in mountain flying. But something had obviously gone terribly wrong. Ground control from all points along his route had lost contact with him, and fifteen hours had blanketed that silence. Nothing at all had been heard from him, and the flight plan he had filed now showed him long overdue for his landing. The direst of tragedies loomed before us.

How do you react to such news at any time, let alone in the middle of the night when search parties are hampered and the world around you is asleep? We could do the only thing we knew to do at such a time, and that was to pray. Several hours went by, and still nothing was heard.

Somewhere around midmorning Barbara was informed that a signal from a downed plane along her husband's route had been detected from a canyon in the mountains. It was indeed Gordon's airplane, and the rescue story was nothing short of a miracle. All three men, when they were found, were alive but badly broken and close to death. They had run into trouble hours before when, making a turn to exit from a blind canyon, they were caught in a downdraft and descended uncontrollably, crashing into trees at the edge of a precipice. Then the hours of silence began.

For Barbara it was the nightmare of living through an unknown tunnel of time, grieving at the possibility of the worst. Questions loomed of losing the love of her life and of raising a young son all alone. For Gordon, as he sat alone with a broken and battered body, his biggest challenge was to stay alive. Undergirding his brokenness, however, was not sadness at the prospect of death but the urgent wish for somebody who could tell his wife he loved her and he was going to make it.

The two experienced diametrically opposite feelings: one born out of living unaware of the truth, the other too wounded to truly feel his pain but fully alert to his longings.

There was only one solution to bring Gordon and Barbara's lives and their feelings hand in hand again: someone who could bring Barbara the knowledge that Gordon was alive and was being rescued and someone who could bind his wounds and mend his body so that he could once again have the capacity to feel in proportion to what he knew and longed for.

Such is the composite the Grand Designer has put into our hearts and minds—the desire to know and the thrill of feeling. For this combination no computer can ever long, and for the lack of this no computer can ever be castigated. How has He made it possible for us to reach such an ideal blend? It is to that we now turn our attention.

An Upward Look

I have always found it intriguing that of all the descriptions God could have given of Himself when referring to His own eternal nature, He chose the metaphor of language. There must have been numerous other possibilities such as love or holiness. Why use the metaphor of language? Is it possible that the only thing that can truly communicate to us other than His person is His Word? Without words life would be inexpressible. Even the best of emotions beg for a verbal expression. That is why the musician reaches not just to the melody but to the romance of language to bring harmony to life.

There is a different explanation between the Hebrew and the Greek in their root concepts when they speak of the *word.* What clearly emerges, though, are the ideas of communication and reason. When John begins his Gospel with the words, "In the beginning was the Word, and the Word was with God, and the Word was God," he without a doubt echoed the very first words of Genesis, "In the beginning, God." But very soon in Genesis 1:3 we also read, "And God said." Right from the beginning God revealed Himself as a God who speaks. He is a communicating God, a God of reason, a God of wisdom—a God who reveals His thoughts.

The gift and privilege of language are distinctively human. To a certain degree the animal world may be brought to a level of understanding dispositions and relationships, but animals are drastically different in kind. A monkey can be trained to dance to music, but it can never learn what it takes to be a Bach or a Handel. Language and reason are the special endowments of humanity, the pinnacle of God's creation. When we cease to understand the role of language we misuse that privilege and can reshape reality just by changing our use of words. All we need to do today to see the utter wrongheadedness of our culture is to see what we have done with words. Words such as *freedom, love, pleasure,* and *marriage* have all lost their meaning. In the beginning was the Word. God has spoken. Language must mirror reality.

From the moment we awaken we start talking to ourselves, and the brain becomes an arena of thought, extracting energy and emotion. With this as a clue let us take the concept of speech and language to find the answer to the place of feeling.

THE LANGUAGE OF GOD

Knowing that our heavenly Father has spoken to us, it is imperative that we understand what He has to say to us about our feelings of joy and pain. The first thing we notice is that He describes Himself as a God who feels. This all-transcending mystery, which we cannot fully grasp, is time and again reiterated in His Word.

In the very first instance that we come upon the strongest of emotions attributed to God we read the words, "The LORD was grieved . . . , and his heart was filled with pain" (Gen. 6:6). Such intensity of feeling seems almost a humanization of God, does it not? We need to be very, very cautious that we do not take the terms in their human limitations and with connotations of finitude, but we will be equally in error to deem these words as purely metaphorical with no real emotion behind them. We are intended to grieve over evil and to rejoice over good.

Somehow, we have been taught to believe that God is so distant that there is nothing in His feelings that bears any analogy to ours. When the Bible tells us that "In the beginning was the Word," it goes on to say, "and the Word was made flesh, and dwelt among us" (John 1:14 KJV). When we trust a person we are told that we can take that person at his or her word. Here in the Gospel of John we see that God's word and being are identical. The incarnate Son of God felt, wept, laughed, and hoped. In the beginning was a thinking, feeling God.

Dennis Kinlaw, one-time president of Asbury College, was once in conversation with me shortly after he had become a grandfather. He told me of the time he held his little grandchild in his arms for the first time and as his eyes flooded with tears wondered, "Is there anyone who feels about me the way I feel about this little one?" The answer was a resounding, "Yes, and even more—God Himself."

But this is where the first very difficult lesson comes. As godlike in their origin as feelings are, we must also learn to put them in perspective and protect ourselves from the glorification of feelings as the final affirmation of truth. God feels with perfect knowledge, and His feeling is in conformity with what is true. He does not act because He feels as much as He acts because He knows. Nothing is so important to the nature of a word as the truth, and truth is the property of propositions not feelings. Feelings are never described as true or false. Feelings may be legitimate or illegitimate, understandable or incomprehensible; but they are not true or false. This is where we often get bogged down, longing for feelings when indeed those very feelings could be the most seductive force to take us away from the truth.

The apostle Peter learned this lesson the hard way when he reveled in the glorious feeling of witnessing what had not been vouchsafed to any other save him, James, and John. I am referring to the transfiguration of our Lord. How marvelous, how inexpressible must have been the awe when they beheld and experienced . . .

the whitest white the eye could ever contain,
the purest bliss the mind could ever imagine,
the greatest theophany one could ever describe,
the most esteemed human personages the Jewish person could ever have wanted to see—Moses and Elijah,
the grandest ecstasy of spirit the heart could ever yearn for
the noblest sound the ears could ever desire when the voice came from heaven, "This is my Son. Listen to Him."

Yet it was in the context of this experience that Peter said what he did about the superiority of the Word.

> We did not follow cleverly invented stories when we told you about the power and coming of our Lord Jesus Christ, but we were eyewitnesses of his majesty. For he received honor and glory from God the Father when the voice came to him from the Majestic Glory, saying, "This is my Son, whom I love; with him I am well pleased." We ourselves heard this voice that came from heaven when we were with him on the sacred mountain.
>
> And we have the word of the prophets made more certain, and you will do well to pay attention to it, as to a light shining in a dark

> place, until the day dawns and the morning star rises in your hearts. Above all, you must understand that no prophecy of Scripture came about by the prophet's own interpretation. For prophecy never had its origin in the will of man, but men spoke from God as they were carried along by the Holy Spirit. (2 Pet. 1:16–21)

Notice wherein lay his certainty—"We have the word of the prophets made more certain." Peter's confidence could very well have been circumscribed in the momentary glow of the transfiguration. In fact, he asked Jesus if they could build their homes right there and not ever descend from the mountain. Is not such the seduction of our own hearts also? Why can we not always feel the constancy of delight? Why must we engage in the battle for survival in the valley? When God is oh! so near, why move to the distance and be subsumed by monotony? Yet, as a wiser man and an older man, Peter saw the experience and the feeling as secondary to the certainty of God's Word, of which Jesus said, "Heaven and earth will pass away, but my words will never pass away" (Matt. 24:35).

Knowing then that His Word is constant and eternal and personally applied, let us discipline our wills and minds to hear from Him each day. There is no greater expression of the will than to choose to hear from His Word on a regular basis. The psalmist said, "Early will I seek thee" (Ps. 63:1 KJV). "Search me, O God, and know . . . my thoughts" (Ps. 139:23 KJV). Samuel said to God, "Speak, LORD, for your servant is listening" (1 Sam. 3:9). Paul cried out to Him at his point of repentance, "What do You want me to do?" (Acts 9:6 NKJV). Our lives are so taken up with speaking that we do very little listening. An expenditure of words without the income of truth leads to spiritual bankruptcy.

It is quite arresting to see how God responded to these prayers. Paul was told of a ministry that would take him before kings and rulers, but he was also warned that he would suffer much for Christ's sake. To such a message, one could legitimately have said to Paul, "And how did that make you feel?" We know very well what Paul said toward the end of his life—"That I may know him, and the power of his resurrection, and the fellowship of his sufferings, being made conformable unto his death" (Phil. 3:10 KJV). Obviously it was not *feeling* that drove Paul but the knowledge of Christ. For Samuel, the message was one that broke his heart. He had a message of judgment to give his predecessor and mentor, Eli.

Listening has a cost, but it has the greatest reward of all, the will of God. Softened as we are by our comforts and by a false idea that serving God is easy and exhilarating, we wonder why He is so far away from us when, in fact, it may be that we are the ones who have left His proximity. We have become so accustomed to hearing preachers or expositors, as important as that is, that many in the process have abandoned the grand privilege of personally hearing from God's Word daily.

WHAT THE LORD CAN DO

Someday I would love to see a series of books describing Scriptures that have changed history, examples of which are profuse. For instance, many are aware of the powerful and devout life of John Wesley. We are told that he preached over forty thousand sermons in his life; he was a prolific writer and wrote volumes that tallied thousands of pages. He traveled nearly a quarter of a million miles in his life, a good percentage of those by horseback. In his eighties he was still preaching twice a day, and in his journal entry at age eighty-six he wrote, "Laziness is slowly creeping in. There is an increasing tendency to stay in bed after five-thirty in the morning."

How incredible is a life so extraordinarily lived! Where did it all begin? It began in a simple service at which the preacher was actually reading from the preface to a commentary on the Book of Romans by Martin Luther. Who would have dreamed at that time that England's history was being shaped by a young preacher whose heart was being strangely warmed under the fire of God's Word?

Martin Luther, who was to change the course of European history, if not world history, was himself unalterably moved and his mind was conquered by that simple little verse from Habakkuk, "The just shall live by his faith" (2:4 KJV). That same verse occurs three more times in the New Testament. Paul wrote it to the greatest of the European churches—Rome. He penned it again to the greatest of the Asian churches—Galatia. And it also appears in the letter to Jewish converts in the Book of Hebrews. The European mind, the Asiatic mind, the Hebrew mind. Anytime something is repeated to this degree and to this breadth, we can be sure there is a world of truth locked into it.

Luther fell under the spell of these words on three distinct occasions. The final moment of reckoning for him came as he literally crawled on his knees up the Lateran staircase in Rome, laboring under the burden of seeking absolution from his sin. Suddenly the meaning of the verse descended on him with life-transforming force, "The just shall live by faith." That telling episode gave him the courage to stand before the powers of his day and withstand their threats. His point of confidence was clear as he stood before their charges. "Here I stand," he said.

In this vein, few stories are as moving as the story of the famed Russian novelist Fyodor Dostoevsky. As he lay dying in February 1881, his daughter said that the last thing he asked for was that the Scriptures be read to him. He asked specifically for the story of the prodigal son. It was that story which had changed his life in his ten-year prison term in Siberia. It is that story which appears in some form in most of his books—the conversion of a derelict. It is little wonder, therefore, that forty thousand young men braved the elements to follow behind his casket in procession as it was carried through the streets of Saint Petersburg—the largest funeral in Russia up to that time—and that Leo Tolstoy bemoaned the death of one of history's greatest personalities. His life was transformed by the Word.

Listen as God speaks. Out of the depths of truth He will tame your passions. Wesley, Luther, and Dostoevsky were men driven by intense passion. They were men who felt issues deeply. More than anything else, they needed to hear from God to guide them in truth. The hymn writer says it so well:

> Lord, I have shut the door,
> Speak now the Word

Which in the din and throng
Could not be heard;
Hushed now my inner heart,
Whisper Thy will,
While I have come apart,
While all is still.

Lord, I have shut the door,
Strengthen my heart;
Yonder awaits the task—I share a part.
Only through grace bestowed
May I be true;
Here, while alone with thee,
My strength renew.[6]

THE LANGUAGE OF SELF

Just as God's Word speaks to us, there must also be the word that we speak to ourselves. Strange as it may seem, this is a vital link to conquering the tug of feeling. Oswald Chambers puts it quite bluntly in his classic volume *My Utmost for His Highest:*

> There are certain things we must not pray about—moods for instance. Moods never go by praying, moods go by kicking. A mood nearly always has its seat in the physical condition, not in the moral. It is a continual effort not to listen to the moods which arise from a physical condition, never to submit to them for a second. We have to take ourselves by the scruff of the neck and shake ourselves, and we will find that we can do what we said we could not. The curse with most of us is that we won't. The Christian life is one of incarnate spiritual pluck.[7]

Chambers goes on to add:

> Unless we train our emotions they will lead us around by the nose, and we will be captives to every passing impulse or reaction. But once faith is trained to control the emotions and knows how to lean resolutely against weaknesses of character, another entryway of doubt is sealed shut forever. Much of our distress as Christians comes not because of sin, but because we are ignorant of the laws of our own nature.

Listen to the way Martin Lloyd-Jones states it. To be sure, at first blush we react against what he is saying and wonder if this is nothing more than autosuggestion. It could be dangerously close to that if it were not also sustained by what the Scriptures teach in identical fashion. First the words of Lloyd-Jones:

> The main art in the matter of spiritual living is to know how to handle yourself. You have to take yourself in hand. You have to address yourself, preach to yourself, question yourself. The essence of this matter is to understand that this self of ours, this other man within us, has got to be handled. Do not listen to him; turn on him; speak to him; condemn him; upbraid him; exhort him; encourage him; remind him of what you know instead of placidly listening to him and allowing him to drag you down and depress you.[8]

Does this all sound strange and rather schizoid? Does not the apostle Paul practice this same discipline? "For my part, I run with a clear goal before me; I am like a boxer who does not beat the air; I bruise my own body and make it know its master" (1 Cor. 9:26–27 NEB). In Psalm 42:5 David asks, "Why are you downcast, O my soul?" In Psalm 116:7, he says, "Be at rest once more, O my soul, for the LORD has been good to you." Certainly, if the apostle Paul's charge that we are to speak to one another with psalms, hymns, and spiritual songs is to encourage and influence, the same must apply to ourselves—making melody in our hearts to the Lord is an encouraging word to ourselves.

THE LANGUAGE OF OBEDIENCE

There is a third source of communication, and that is the language of obedience, which in turn builds and strengthens faith. We all know that our faith results in works, but we often forget that the reverse is also true. One of the fundamental differences between the Greek way of thinking and the Hebrew way of thinking was that for the Greeks truth came by reason, and for the Hebrews truth came by obedience.

We see this several times in the Scriptures. Moses, Ezekiel, Hosea, and Jonah did not feel like doing what God had asked them to do. In fact, every heartbeat within them was impelling them to do otherwise. Yet God said they were to obey. The remedy was not to do God's will because they felt like doing it, but just to do it and their faith would be strengthened.

A classic demonstration of this principle was seen in the encounter between God and Moses. When Moses demanded proof that God had indeed called him, God said, "I will be with you. And this will be the sign to you that it is I who have sent you: When you have brought the people out of Egypt, you will worship God on this mountain" (Exod. 3:12). The proof of God's call was *after* the obedience, not before.

This language of obedience may be the most difficult of all the languages we speak, one that rises above our feelings but utters volumes of faith. Of all the surprise that awaits one in a marital relationship this is one of the bigger and more difficult ones to accept and follow. Here I pay tribute to my wife in a way that is hard to fully represent with justice, but anyone in this situation will know whereof I speak. There are times when a difference might arise between us, due to pride or just an obstinate will that does not want to look weak and stands in the way of making things right. I can only say to my embarrassment that even as I have struggled I have watched her stand tall at those times, and I have seen the triumph of her love vanquish any dark and petty inclination. She is never afraid to reach out and to resist the ugly trap of stubbornness. Such are the glorious lessons of faith itself. We do, we obey, we yield, we submit to God, even when our natural inclination wants to drag us in the opposite direction.

Was not this the triumph of faith in the lives of Shadrach, Meshach, and Abednego? Under the threat of death they stood their ground and were sure that God would deliver them. "But even if he does not," they said, "we want you to know, O king, that we will not serve your gods or worship the image of gold you have set up" (Dan. 3:18). I suggest that our secular society has lost its ability to feel God because it has lost its ability to obey Him.

THE LANGUAGE OF FRIENDS

Fourth, there is a language that comes to us through friends. One of the treasured gifts of God in life is the gift of friendship. This gift comes as His grace because I have seen it manifested even when the recipient is undeserving. Over the years as I have traveled and sat at meals with people around the world, I have carried away with me this beautiful gift. On every continent I have memories, enriched beyond measure, of some friend who at some time shared with me the gift of hospitality. When feelings are down and the road seems desolate, it is the friend who carries us along.

One of the more sobering moments in Israel's history was when Absalom betrayed his father, David, and sought to overthrow him. But the darker part of that episode was that the counsel that lurked behind the scenes came from Ahithophel, a one-time confidant of David's. It was that tragedy that lingered long in the heart of David. The heartache must have come up again and again for him. In the fifty-fifth Psalm David referred to it: "If an enemy were insulting me, I could endure it; if a foe were raising himself against me, I could hide from him. But it is you, a man like myself, my companion, my close friend, with whom I once enjoyed sweet fellowship as we walked with the throng at the house of God" (Ps. 55:12–14). Again he mentioned it in the forty-first Psalm: "Even my close friend, whom I trusted, he who shared my bread, has lifted up his heel against me" (Ps. 41:9).

When I was a student in college, a handful of us made a covenant with each other to pray for one another regularly. Over the years our ways have taken us far apart in distance. One of those friends was a young man of extraordinary courage, Koos Fietje, who went as a missionary to Thailand with Overseas Missionary Fellowship. In 1974 I was passing through Bangkok en route to speak in Cambodia. Though I had wanted so much to see Koos, I did not want to inconvenience him by asking him to journey to Bangkok from up-country. I was to spend only one night there anyway, and so I made no prior contact. As I picked up my bags from the baggage carousel in the airport and walked through the glass door, who should be standing there but Koos. He reached out and grabbed my hand and said, "You thought you would slip by, didn't you?" To this day I cannot recall how he knew I was passing through.

We spent that whole night in the hotel room talking about how God was leading us in our lives and of His call to us to be faithful. He exhorted me to stay on track. He was an extraordinary man. But I knew that Koos was really troubled, and as we parted he repeated what he had said a few times, that perhaps he would pay with his life for the boldness of his witness for Christ. Sure enough, I would not see Koos again. A few short years later, as he was coming out of a prayer meeting in the city where he ministered, a man shot him to death at point-blank range.

God gave me the privilege of a godly friend. Many times when I have struggled with the feelings and strains that come with the itinerant life, Koos's martyrdom has spurred me on. Through life or by death, a friend can help conquer many a wrong and petty feeling.

Paul said in his letter to the Philippians: "It is right for me to feel this way about all of you, since I have you in my heart; for whether I am in chains or defending and confirming the gospel, all of you share in God's grace with me. God can testify how I long for all of you with the affection of Christ Jesus" (1:7–8). That is a testimony to the friendship of God's people for a servant of Christ in chains.

THE LANGUAGE OF THE CHURCH

We come at last to the place of the church in caring for its people and in undergirding those in need. The church ought to be a place for inner healing and restoration. Here the patience of Christ and the wisdom of a disciplined life is needed to instruct and guide. When a person stumbles or is taken in sin it is the privileged call of the church of Christ to reach out and to help restore. When one struggles with feelings that God is so far away, the arms of those who are part of the church will be the only arms God has to draw such people near. When someone feels abandoned, the hearts of the people of God may be the only hearts God can tap to feel with this person.

Nothing brings back feelings of being cared for as much as being in a community that feels. There is hurt and loneliness on a rampant scale today. Nothing will speak to our society as much as a community that reaches out with the love of Christ.

But there is a second way in which the church has a role today that we cannot fully comprehend. It is the role of music. Few avenues are at the same time as powerful and as vulnerable in controlling feelings. Listen even as a youth culture throbs and gyrates under the pulsating sound—not to say, often the noise—of some styles of music. One cannot help but ask some hard questions about this phenomenon. What is such music doing to the listeners' feelings, and what is it possibly revealing about their inner state? I do know from good friends who are professional musicians that they have some serious concerns, too.

But rather than risk all that such questions entail, let us simply make note of one thing. With the passing of years, music plays a greater role in consolation and inspiration than it does in vibration and ecstasy. Over time, the heart gives way to certain cries: the cry for peace and tranquillity, the search for solace and succor, the cry that does not just carry hope for the future but reflects on the past. I am more convinced than ever that music has the capacity to strike at the core of our beings in a way that God has designed our beings to respond. Music will bring either harmony or discord and, more often, reveals the harmony or discord in a life.

One of the most valuable roles music plays is to build the reservoir of our memories. It serves as a rewind button that brings back the past in a fond remembrance. In that sense, it helps connect life's dreams to life's accomplishments. That is why the church must think through carefully the blessing and the caution that comes from the proliferation of new choruses and songs now upon us. We are leaving many in their middle years severed from their musical past. Songs they loved to sing are no longer part of their church's worship, and when change is constant there is not time even for the young to build up their memory banks. Music has an extraordinary role to play in the church, and it is a privileged means of touching our feelings for the good.

As we come to end this journey of talking to our feelings, let me summarize the truths. We must hear the voice of God speaking to us through His Word. We pause to speak to ourselves about what we know to be true. We speak the language of obedience to our emotions. We build friendships that endure and strengthen us when we are weak. We draw from the strength of the church to sustain us, and we enjoy the sound and the inspiration of music that God has given to His people.

Nothing illustrated this five-fold strength to me as clearly as a Sunday morning service a few months ago. My father-in-law had suffered a heart attack and had been diagnosed as needing heart bypass surgery. But, with the demands upon the medical system, he was told that it could be seven to nine months before his turn came up. He was sure he would not survive the wait and was coping with the prospect of death.

As he rested at home on that particular Sunday, his wife was in church, as faithful in being part of God's family as they have always been throughout their lives. I observed her from a distance during the entire service. Her friends around her asked about his condition. The sermon, the prayers, the truths from the pulpit, all carried some application for her situation. She held her composure through it all. Then came the closing hymn, and the tears could no longer be contained. Possibly no one else tied into its truths the way she did:

> Be still, my soul, the Lord is on thy side;
> Bear patiently the cross of grief or pain;
> Leave to thy God to order or provide;

In every change He faithful will remain.
Be still, my soul, thy best, thy heavenly Friend
Through thorny ways leads to a joyful end.

Be still my soul, thy God doth undertake
To guide the future as He has the past.
Thy hope, thy confidence let nothing shake;
All now mysterious shall be bright at last.
Be still, my soul, the waves and winds still know
His voice who ruled them while He dwelt below.

Be still, my soul, the hour is hastening on
When we shall be forever with the Lord,
When disappointment, grief, and fear are gone,
Sorrow forgot, love's purest joys restored.
Be still, my soul, when change and tears are past,
All safe and blessed we shall meet at last.[9]

How gracious it was of God to meet her in that need. All languages converged to bring a calmness to the soul. There remains only one question. How does one reach the assurance of such truths and the peace they bring? Or, put differently, how can we be led by the truth and not by our feelings?

CONCLUSION

I have thought of this long and hard as I have reflected on the inner struggle when one says, "I have tried everything but cannot feel God." The well-known singing group U2 has a song entitled "I Still Haven't Found What I'm Looking For." The lyrics take you through all that life has to offer and even refers to the gospel but ends with a "been there, done that" refrain—"I still haven't found what I'm looking for." On the basis of all the thinking I have done on this legitimate quandary, I have drawn two conclusions.

The first is that, one way or the other, as we live we will be broken; we will *have* to be broken. We will either be broken by a lie or by the truth. Even Jesus embodied and very dramatically showed this certainty in one very significant choice. This choice lies at the heart of what God's nearness and farness are all about, but we do not give it due reflection. When He came face to face with the cross, He knew what lay before Him, and He knew that any path He chose was going to deeply wound Him. An anguished cry came from within Him indicating how He eschewed that moment. He asked His disciples to stay close to Him. He needed their nearness. "Could you men not keep watch with me for one hour?" He said, as they slept while His troubled soul cried out in Gethsemane (Matt. 26:40). His prayer, "My Father, if it is possible, let this cup pass me by . . ." (Matt. 26:39 NEB) catches us all off guard until He adds, "Not my will, but thine, be done" (Luke 22:42 KJV).

What was the dread? Certainly not the physical pain. He could face that. It was the knowledge and the feeling of being abandoned by even God the Father *while at the same time being in the center of God's will.* God would not be near during that eternal transaction but would turn His back upon His Son. Thus, it was He who on the cross cried, "My God, My God, why have You forsaken Me?" (Matt. 27:46 NKJV).

Here is the point: In an effort to forestall the rupture with His Father, Jesus could have walked away from that sacrifice, but in so doing He would have actually ended up being alienated from His Father's will and heart. By choosing to die and endure that momentary separation He was drawn completely into the bosom of the Father. Putting it differently, He had a choice—to resist the cross and leave the world a broken place, or else to be broken Himself so that the world might be drawn near and live. In that death and separation from the consolation of His Father, He was able to bring us who were far off into the embrace of God.

That cross on which our Lord was broken, where He took our sin and suffering, where He took our alienation, where He was abandoned by all, that cross is at the heart of the gospel. If it is properly understood and surrendered to, the cross cannot just merit a "been there, done that, didn't work" kind of feeling. The one who is not a follower of Jesus Christ wonders where God is in this hurting world. Why does He seem so far off? We often think that one who does not know Christ does not understand what the cross actually means. And in a very real sense this is true. But I dare to make a suggestion, and this is where I have come to my second conclusion. Even though the cross is so foreign to the skeptics and to humanity's normal way of thinking, somewhere deep in their own hearts they unwittingly affirm its underlying message that even in the most evil expressions of life God must be somewhere within reach. Two illustrations will sustain this and will bring us to a vital point of decision.

Elie Wiesel, Nobel Prize winner and Jewish survivor of the Holocaust, tells of the time when he was in a concentration camp and was compelled, along with a few others, to witness the hanging of two Jewish men and one Jewish boy. The two men died quite instantly, but the dying of the young lad for some reason became protracted as he struggled for half an hour on the gallows.

Somebody behind Wiesel was heard to mutter, "Where is God? Where is He?" Then the voice ground out the anguish again, "Where is He?"

Wiesel also felt the question irrepressibly springing from within him: "Where is God? Where is He?"

Then he heard a voice softly within him saying, "He is hanging there on the gallows."

Author Dennis Ngien, in his article "The God Who Suffers," added a footnote to that story. He quoted theologian Jurgen Moltmann saying that any other answer would be blasphemy.[10]

I ask the question, Can any faith other than Christianity answer that question in its fullest sense? As we look around at the feelingless atrocities we wonder, Where is God? And the answer comes: He is right in the middle—at the receiving end of our atrocities.

These very unconscionable and pitiful acts of blowing up a building and thus killing men, women, and children and of suffocating a newborn baby are acts against Him. We inflict pain on other people because we have rejected Him first. I find that illustration of Wiesel utterly amazing. Where is God? Right there in that building. Right there in that plastic bag. The cross somehow invades us as the only reasonable point of definition for a wounded world. God is on the gallows Himself, so that we might come near. Any other answer is blasphemous.

From this truth follows a very significant personal challenge. When we come face to face with the cross, we have a choice to make: We either recognize its implications and bring ourselves, our passions, and all that we are, to be crucified with Christ so that we might live within the sound of His voice and the feel of His heart, or we walk away from the cross and live feeling alienated from God. But this is where the lie comes in—believing that we can be close to the Father without dying to ourselves. In Christ's own ministry this was impossible. We hear so much about "coming to Christ." We hear too little of being crucified with Him. When we come to Him with all of our past baggage, nothing will change if we do not let that old self be crucified.

Something has to die, either the lie to which the feelings are subject, or the truth to which the feelings must conform. That is at the heart of what must happen in being crucified with Him. I contend that in a subtle way the world sees the reality of the cross here, too. There is a contemporary illustration that speaks volumes for my contention.

In an article in *Ladies' Home Journal* some time ago, the writer bemoaned the loss of ethics in our time but suggested that there were occasional hints of light to tell us there is hope. As proof of that optimism she told the story of David Kaczynski. For many years the man nicknamed The Unabomber wreaked havoc and fear in the senseless killings he carried out. When he was finally tracked down, an incredible act of courage was uncovered behind the efforts of police to find him. As David Kaczynski, just an ordinary person, followed the media profiles of who this killer could be, a horrible thought struck him. Every clue from the profile being given pointed to his brother, Ted. Finally, fear-stricken, David went to the police to give his reasons for believing that Ted Kaczynski might be the one they were looking for. The police followed through, and the wheels of justice are now grinding out the horror of this irrational spate of killings that Ted Kaczynski is charged with.[11]

One has to wonder what went on in David Kaczynski's mind when he first suspected that his brother might be the murderer. We do know that when the conviction in his mind was certain, he had to be willing to turn his brother in, knowing that it could lead to his brother's death. But no, let's stop here. It was not the brother's death that was the battle. The real battle was within David Kaczynski. Was he willing to die to his own personal desire, even his love for his brother, that the truth might win and righteousness have the day? After a life-defining struggle, he died to his own desires so that the killing would stop. That was the choice he nobly made. In so doing, truth clasped the hand of feeling and led it to triumph. In principle, the deaths of Mary Jane and Gary Chauncey so that their daughter, Audrey, could live reveal the same thing—death to self.

Can we do any less in our commitment to Christ? The apostle Paul exemplified this truth in a very simple statement to Timothy: "I know whom I have believed, and am convinced that he is able to guard what I have entrusted to him for that day" (2 Tim. 1:12). There is an equally simple way to illustrate this and bring this study to a close.

If you were seated in an airport with your suitcase beside you and you left for a moment to talk to someone else, what would you do if, during your absence, your suitcase were stolen? You might go over to the desk and ask the agent if he or she could track it down for you. The answer would most probably be no. When it was in your charge and you lost it, you would have no recourse with the airline.

If, on the other hand, you had checked it in with the airline and upon arrival at your destination found it was not there, you would have every right to ask the airline's agent where it was. He or she would immediately begin a search for your lost luggage. You see, the airline is only responsible for what you have committed to it. They are not responsible for what you have not committed to them.

This is precisely what the apostle Paul meant here. He was confident that God would guard what had been entrusted to Him. Bring your feelings to the cross. Entrust them into His care, and He will guard them for you.

Three

The Cry for a Reason in Suffering

WITH THESE WORDS, the eighteenth-century Scottish skeptic David Hume summed up humanity's greatest obstacle to believing that God exists:

> Were a stranger to drop suddenly into this world, I would show him as a specimen of its ills a hospital full of diseases, a prison crowded with malefactors and debtors, a field strewn with carcasses, a fleet floundering in the ocean, a nation languishing under tyranny, famine or pestilence. Honestly, I don't see how you can possibly square with an ultimate purpose of love.[1]

Yet another says this:

> It is not science that has led me to doubt the purpose of God. It is the state of the world. It is the pitiful unending struggle for existence among the nations. It is the collapse of our idealisms before the brute facts of force and chaos. It is the feeling that there is something demonic in the heart of things which is working

> against us; that there is a radical twist in the very constitution of the universe which will always defeat man's hopes, make havoc of his dreams and bring his pathetic optimism crashing in disaster. Purpose? Look at the world. That settles it.[2]

In Fyodor Dostoevsky's masterpiece *The Brothers Karamazov,* Ivan Karamazov says:

> Tell me yourself—I challenge you: let's assume that you were called upon to build the edifice of human destiny so that men would finally be happy and would find peace and tranquility. If you knew that, in order to attain this, you would have to torture just one single creature, let's say the little girl who beat her chest so desperately in the outhouse, and that on her unavenged tears you could build that edifice, would you agree to do it? Tell me and don't lie![3]

It is very hard not to have some sympathy with the skepticism expressed here and with the question that is raised. (The particular slant of Ivan Karamazov's question is more complex, and therefore, I have added a postscript at the end of the book to respond to it in greater depth.) The abundance of evil, and the extent to which so much of it seems apparently gratuitous, compels the thinking person to question the coexistence of a good God with a world of evil. Which of us has not looked at a deformed child, swallowed hard with pity, and pondered the purpose behind it? Which of us has seen a mother who has lost her child and not wondered why? To live is to sooner or later experience or witness pain and suffering. To reason is to inevitably ponder "Why?"

I do not know of any question that is asked more, nor of any obstacle to belief that is more persistent. The best of the prophets raised this very issue, with different slants. Habakkuk asked, "Why do you make me look at injustice? Why do you tolerate wrong?" (Hab. 1:3). David cried out, "How long will the enemy mock you?" (Ps. 74:10). Jonah was exasperated by the violence of the Ninevites and wanted them wiped out. Jeremiah challenged the Lord, saying, "I would speak with you about your justice: Why does the way of the wicked prosper?" (Jer. 12:1).

I have never been in a conversation with a skeptic who failed to raise this as the principal reason for his or her skepticism. The number of those who have ceased to believe in God because of the death of a loved one or the maiming of a friend is legion. The question is without doubt one of the most honest and genuine questions that can be raised of a Christian faith that talks of a loving God who is in control of all things.

Unfortunately, glib and incoherent answers to such heart cries have resulted in a breakdown of communication between honest skeptics who are seekers of the truth and those who claim to know it. We often dismiss the questioner as one who does not want to believe and, hence, finds a reason for his or her unbelief. There may be many who are determined to disbelieve, but there are also those for whom the mind and heart wrestle sincerely with the problem. Someone has put it more succinctly: Virtue in distress and vice in triumph make atheists of mankind.

But if the Christian can be charged with ignoring the genuineness of the questioner, the questioner must also face the indicting possibility that he or she has often not thought through the question fairly. There is a blatant oversight that often accompanies this challenge to the mind, and that is that the skeptics who have raised the question must also give an answer to the same question. How do *they* explain the problem of pain? Not only must they give an answer, but they must ultimately justify the very question itself—all that, while leaving God out of the picture. Here the voices get silent and their own answers border on the irrational.

G. K. Chesterton summed up this counterpoint well when he said, "When belief in God becomes difficult, the tendency is to turn away from Him; but in heaven's name to what?" The Christian does not deny that a meaningful answer must be found, but has the one who denies God found a better answer to the problem of evil? With a touch of humor, and in recognition that many answers come close but not close enough, Chesterton went on to say, "My problem with life is not that it is rational, nor that it is irrational . . . but that it is almost rational." Just when we are able to form a cohesive framework, someone or something pokes a hole in it, and we take a step back.

The Bible does not ignore this question in silence but addresses it with great seriousness. Possibly the most misunderstood yet oft-quoted book that deals with the question of human pain and suffering is the Book of Job. His name has become synonymous with suffering, and yet so few have chosen to systematically weigh out his arguments. When we consider how old this book is we ought to be fascinated by how profound is his treatment of the subject.

It is my hope that we can dig deep and mine the arguments that provide the only viable answer to this mystery that plagues us all. But before we enter into that quest, let us at least face the question forthrightly in its philosophical ramifications. This will have to be brief and will demand immense concentration, but we must put the question in context. Once we get past this philosophical hurdle, our answers will be felt with greater force.

QUESTIONING THE QUESTION

Some years ago I was speaking at the University of Nottingham, England, when a rather exasperated person in the audience made his attack upon God with this very question. C. S. Lewis reminds us that there is nothing so self-defeating as a question that is not fully understood when it is fully posed. This questioner was felled by his own question.

"There cannot possibly be a God," he said, "with all the evil and suffering that exists in the world!" I asked him if we could interact on this issue for a few moments. He agreed.

"When you say there is such a thing as evil, are you not assuming that there is such a thing as good?" I asked.

"Of course," he retorted.

"But when you assume there is such a thing as good, are you not also assuming that there is such a thing as a moral law on the basis of which to distinguish between good and evil?"

"I suppose so," came the hesitant and much softer reply.

This was an extremely important point to note as I made the argument. Most skeptics have never given this point a thought. I therefore reminded this questioner, in his initial hesitancy, of the debate between the agnostic Bertrand Russell and the Christian philosopher Frederick Copleston. During the debate, Copleston asked Russell if he believed in good and bad. Russell admitted that he did, and Copleston responded by asking him how he differentiated between the two. Russell said that he differentiated between good and bad in the same way that he distinguished between colors.

"But you distinguish between colors by seeing, don't you?" Copleston reminded Russell. "How then, do you judge between good and bad?"

"On the basis of feeling, what else?" came Russell's sharp reply.[4]

Somebody should have interrupted and told Russell that in some cultures they loved their neighbors while in other cultures they ate them—both on the basis of feeling. Did Mr. Russell have a personal preference?

How in the name of reason can we possibly justify differentiating between good and bad on the basis of feeling? Whose feeling? Hitler's or Mother Teresa's? In other words, there must be a moral law, a standard by which to determine good and bad. How else can one make the determination? My questioner finally granted that assumption without hesitation.

So let me retrace for a moment how far he had come. I had asked him if he believed in good; he answered yes. But if he believed in good, he had to grant a moral law by which to distinguish between the two. He agreed.

"If, then, there is a moral law," I said, "you must posit a moral lawgiver. But that is who you are trying to disprove and not prove. If there is no moral lawgiver, there is no moral law. If there is no moral law, there is no good. If there is no good, there is no evil. I am not sure what your question is!"

There was silence, and then he said, "What, then, am I asking you?"

The momentary humor was inescapable. He was visibly shaken that at the heart of his question lay an assumption that contradicted his conclusion. This is exactly what I meant when I said that the skeptic not only had to give an answer to his or her own question but also had to justify the question. And even as the laughter subsided I reminded him that I accepted the question, but that his question justified my assumptions that this was a moral universe, not his. For if God is not the author of life, neither *good* nor *bad* is a meaningful term.

This constantly eludes the skeptic who seems to think that by raising the question of evil a trap has been sprung to destroy theism when, in fact, the very raising of the question ensnares the skeptic who raised the question. A hidden assumption comes into the open. In other words, can we really raise a problem with moral implications if this is not a moral universe? The moment we use the word *better,* said C. S. Lewis, we assume a point of reference.

In the same vein, are we positing a legitimate category when we ask why this universe seems immoral if the universe itself has no moral basis or reason for being? The disorienting reality to those who raise the problem of evil is that the Christian can be consistent when he or she talks about the problem of evil and gives a coherent response to it, while the skeptic is hard-pressed to respond to the question of good in an amoral universe. In short, the problem of evil is not solved by doing away with the existence of God in the face of evil; the problem of evil and suffering must be resolved while keeping God in the picture.

This was precisely Job's conclusion. He never once lost sight of the fact that God was very much in control. But he could not reconcile this with his theological framework. He had always assumed that if you are good you will be blessed and if you are bad you would be cursed. Why, when he had been good, was he being cursed? His theology was tottering, not his belief in God.

The way Job worked through this problem makes for a fascinating study, and to that we will give our attention.

A Strange Beginning

In the first chapter of the book, we find Job facing one calamity after another. He lost his health, his wealth, and finally, his family. As he sat on his ash pile, covered from head to toe with boils, his wife said to him, "Are you still holding on to your integrity? Curse God and die!"

But Job replied, "You are talking like a foolish woman. Shall we accept good from God, and not trouble?" The Bible adds, "In all this, Job did not sin in what he said" (Job 2:9–10).

One has to both understand and at the same time wonder what Job's wife really meant by "curse God and die." If God exists, does cursing Him accomplish anything? One may as well put on a pair of sneakers and kick a tank. If, however, God does not exist, who would Job really have been cursing? But let us give her the benefit of the doubt. She was reacting the way every human being is tempted to react when everything he or she has believed in seems to make absolutely no sense in the face of what appears to be the opposite.

On the other hand, Job made an assumption, too, that just as God is the source of comfort, so also was He the source of pain, and therefore, he just had to resign himself to it. Was Job correct? Let us bear in mind that we are given a glimpse of the prologue and what preceded this test, of which Job had no knowledge. But in the epilogue we see Job understanding the big picture, and the pattern that emerged brought much consolation and worship into his heart. Through the long process of his numerous conversations, the questions he asked became clearer and gained very sharp focus. That may have been one of Job's greatest discoveries—how important it was to ask the right questions.

As we read on, we are told that Job's three friends, Eliphaz, Bildad, and Zophar, journeyed to see him in order to help him understand where God was in all of his devastation. (I have always insisted that they could not have possibly found their names from a baby book. I used to also say that I have never met anybody with those names, but that changed when I met a Bildad somewhere in some distant part of this globe.)

One can imagine their conversations as they traveled to see Job and laid their plans in place, determining who would play what role in their goal to bring him comfort. But one brief glimpse of his pitiful state left them speechless. They remained conspicuously silent for seven days and seven nights. Without doubt, they were at their wisest and best when they were silent. As much as one appreciates these men for their concern in coming to Job, one is mystified at their insensitivity in this, their friend's most excruciating hour. They gave only what we would call "canned answers" and unthought-through theological pronouncements that on the surface seemed sound but were vacuous in the face of Job's agony.

The first to open his mouth was Eliphaz. He was the oldest and the kindest. But of all the reasoning he could have brought to bear on his counsel, he narrated the strangest episode.

> A word was secretly brought to me,
>   my ears caught a whisper of it.
> Amid disquieting dreams in the night,
>   when deep sleep falls on men,
> fear and trembling seized me
>   and made all my bones shake.
> A spirit glided past my face,
>   and the hair on my body stood on end.
> It stopped,
>   but I could not tell what it was.
> A form stood before my eyes,
>   and I heard a hushed voice:
> "Can a mortal be more righteous than God?
>   Can a man be more pure than his Maker? . . ."
> We have examined this, and it is true.
>   So hear it and apply it to yourself. (Job 4:12–17; 5:27)

One can only imagine what Job felt while Eliphaz waxed eloquent about this dreamy experience of his. But Job paid him the courtesy of listening to his speech before erupting in dismay. He painfully pleaded for understanding on the depth of his loss:

> If only my anguish could be weighed
> and all my misery be placed on the scales!
> It would surely outweigh the sand of the seas. . . .
> The arrows of the Almighty are in me,
> my spirit drinks in their poison;
> God's terrors are marshaled against me. . . .
> A despairing man should have the devotion of his friends. (Job 6:1–4, 14)

There is no evident flaw to Eliphaz's thoughts except for the questionable foundation on which he built them. He called to mind Job's "creatureliness" and, hence, his sinfulness. He argued for the justice of God and the fairness with which He deals with people. There is no evident flaw to Eliphaz's thoughts, except for the weird foundation on which he built it and his apparent callousness, which seemed to care more for the eloquence of the argument than for the misery of his friend.

I remember in the early years of my ministry when I was being asked by a couple why God allows suffering in our lives. I sat facing them as they remained in the last pew of the church after everyone had gone. As I leaned forward to respond to their question I suddenly noticed their baby lying beside them, obviously born with Down's syndrome. I mentally stepped back for a moment. I knew then that their question struck deep into the heart. This was not an academic question. Their feelings were real, and so my answer needed to be.

Put yourself in Job's predicament. With everything you cherished gone, what would you think of a friend who talked about a dream he had where a spirit glided past his face and stood still? His hair stood on end out of shock and then the spirit spoke to him with an answer to your pain, "Can a man be pure before his Maker?" One could forgive Job if he exploded with sheer frustration and said, "What on earth are you talking about?"

Let me note that it is not important whether Eliphaz's dream really took place. The real question is how someone else could determine if that whole episode was really true. And even if it were, it was at best a personal encounter for Eliphaz. Is it then wise to build an entire theological system on an aberrant experience that cannot be verified by anyone else? He still needed to tread softly around Job's anguish, and evidently Eliphaz did not.

I am reminded of my days in graduate studies when I had the privilege of studying under a very brilliant scholar. He was short on patience and long on outbursts if any student dared to present any material that was deemed unworthy. In one major test he gave that was particularly difficult, every one of us students prayed for just a passing grade. One student, not having the faintest clue to what one of the questions meant, dared to pad his answers with weighty verbiage, hoping that somewhere in the volume of words he would hint in the direction of an appropriate answer. When he got his paper back, written across it was what I think to be one of the funniest one-liners I have ever read. The professor had simply written, "This is not right. . . . This is not even wrong!" It took a long moment, but the student got the point.

You see, there are at least three things one can say to the answer given to any question that is posed. One is to say that it is right. Another is to say that it is wrong. The third is to say that it has not even risen to the dignity of an error. For to say that something is wrong is to at least concede that something meaningful has been said.

How does one respond to a dream or a vision when there is nothing to corroborate the assertion being made? At the risk of being rude, how do we know that Eliphaz was not merely hallucinating or suffering from some kind of messianic complex?

How much the Christian faith has suffered at the hands of those for whom a highly charged emotional experience from the sidebar existence of life is made the sole interpreter of the main script of everyone else's existence. There seems to be no way to "test the spirits" anymore, and all that is needed for a church or group to be formed is the acceptance or allowance of any kind of manifestation, with suspicion being the only inadmissible element. This is a dangerous way to claim devotion to God, because there is no way to differentiate between worshiping God and playing God.

As authentic as Eliphaz's experience may have been, Job is well within his rights to dismiss it. "A despairing man should have the devotion of his friends. . . . But my brothers are as undependable as intermittent streams, as the streams that overflow when darkened by thawing ice and swollen with melting snow, but that cease to flow in the dry season" (Job 6:14–15). They offered a drink when no one had need of it but denied that same drink to one who was dying of thirst. Eliphaz's speech missed Job's anguish. Job goes on to ask God:

> Teach me, and I will be quiet;
> show me where I have been wrong.
> How painful are honest words!
> But what do your arguments prove?
> Do you mean to correct what I say,
> and treat the words of a despairing man as wind?
> You would even cast lots for the fatherless
> and barter away your friend.
> But now be so kind as to look at me. (Job 6:24–28)

With unapologetic forthrightness, Job questions Eliphaz's heartlessness. In effect, he calls him an unmoved storehouse of words. No feeling. No reason. Just a dispassionate spouter of platitudes.

A Prophet of the Wind

Their stalemate prepared the way for Job's next friend, Bildad. He wasted no time and immediately said to Job:

> Your words are a blustering wind. . . .
> Ask the former generations
> and find out what their fathers learned,

for we were born only yesterday and know nothing. . . .
Will they not instruct you and tell you?
    Will they not bring forth words from their understanding?
    (Job 8:2, 8–10)

No one can read Bildad's response and question anything he said. Yet somehow there is something wrong that is not easily identifiable. The thoughts themselves seem very true—after all, what is wrong with saying that we are to give ear to the wisdom of the ages? Former generations have much to teach us with respect to suffering and pain. The wealth of poetry and prose that has been written over the centuries in the stormy moments of life has shed light for many when they have had to cross through such dark valleys.

I think, for example, of the powerful testimony of a woman named Annie Johnston Flint. She was one who lived most of her life in pain. Orphaned early in life, her body was embarrassed by incontinence, weakened by cancer, and twisted and deformed by rheumatoid arthritis. She was incapacitated for so long that according to one eyewitness she needed seven or eight pillows around her body just to cushion the raw sores she suffered from being bedridden. Yet her autobiography is rightly called *The Making of the Beautiful.* Almost like a minstrel from heaven she penned words that touch the heart in its despairing moments. One of her best-known poems, put to music, reads:

He giveth more grace when the burdens grow greater,
He sendeth more strength when the labors increase;
To added affliction, He addeth His mercy,
To multiplied trials His multiplied peace.

When we have exhausted our store of endurance,
When our strength has failed e're the day is half done,
When we reach the end of our hoarded resources
Our Father's full giving has only begun.

His love has no limit, His grace has no measure,

His power has no boundary known unto men;
For out of His infinite riches in Jesus
He giveth, and giveth, and giveth again![5]

One is tempted to ascribe a sense of divine inspiration to words as soul-stirring and to sentiments as profound as these, uttered by a life as broken as hers. I have little doubt that over the years many have turned to this hymn time and again and drawn comfort from her words.

The question here, however, is whether these words provide an answer to the question of why pain occurs in our lives, or do they merely echo the sentiments of acceptance and triumph in the situation? Job pondered on the reason for his suffering more than he did on how to endure it. Beyond the poetry of triumph we can look back upon the exhortations of those who have thought this problem through, and once again we come away with a mixed response. From a voice in antiquity like that of Augustine to the more recent voice of C. S. Lewis, wisdom is offered on this gnawing subject. The words of Malcolm Muggeridge sustain this good news/bad news feeling. He said:

> Contrary to what might be expected, I look back on experiences that at the time seemed especially desolating and painful, with particular satisfaction. Indeed, I can say with complete truthfulness that everything I have learned in my seventy-five years in this world, everything that has truly enhanced and enlightened my existence, has been through affliction and not through happiness, whether pursued or attained. In other words, if it ever were to be possible to eliminate affliction from our earthly existence by means of some drug or other medical mumbo jumbo . . . the result would not be to make life delectable, but to make it too banal or trivial to be endurable. This of course is what the cross signifies, and it is the cross more than anything else, that has called me inexorably to Christ.[6]

There is a gold mine of truth in these thoughts Muggeridge has expressed. But to the one in despair, this too may seem a distant answer to the more proximate agony. Hence, the response from Job to Bildad revealed his exasperation. He asked, "How can a mortal be righteous before God?" (Job 9:2). God's power seemed so arbitrary, Job charged—He makes mountains and then moves them at His own will. Once again, Job did not doubt God's existence; he merely asked to know His purpose. Then he uttered with great longing a cry that began to open the door just a fraction: "If only there were someone to arbitrate between [God and me]" (Job 9:33).

A Voice of Anger

We begin, at this point, to see Job's own journey crystallizing. In the first instance, he asked for instruction. Now he is asking for arbitration or a point of contact. Into his world that is broken on the outside comes a gradual rebuilding from within.

Then came the third voice—that of Zophar. The youngest and rudest of the three, he basically called Job an idiot and a windbag. "It is more likely that a donkey will give birth to a human being than for you to listen to wisdom," said Zophar (see Job 11:12).

It is somewhat humorous to note how human nature expressed itself in a situation like this centuries ago and comforting to realize that those characters were no different than we are. Impatience and anger are predictable when you think you have the answer and the other person fails to see your point. Eliphaz, Bildad, and Zophar saw themselves as God-sent emissaries with nuggets of wisdom in abundance. Job was mystified at their utter thoughtlessness.

In essence, Zophar's answer was that God's ways were not Job's ways and Job just needed to understand that. But was that really an answer? The fact is that the devil's ways were not Job's ways, either, and that was already clear to him. His question concerned the *what* and *why* of the difference between God's thinking and his, not just the fact of it.

Now the point of clarity begins. Earlier Job had begged for someone to teach him. Then he asked if there was a mediator to settle his dispute with God. Next he cried out in desperation, asking, "If a man dies, will he live again?" (Job 14:14). If nothing else, pain at least helps us clarify the question. From his hunger to know the reason why, to his question of life beyond the grave, Job had come a long way.

The Illusion of Omniscience

God began to answer Job's question. He had, in effect, listened in silence, waiting for this conversation to unfold and giving the best of minds an opportunity to try to untangle the mystery. None of them seemed to feel what Job felt, and over a period of days their thoughts were bringing a deeper wedge between them and Job. As God began His discourse He challenged Job to face up to the heart of the matter. Job had long waited for this.

> Who is this that darkens my counsel
> with words without knowledge?
> Brace yourself like a man;
> I will question you,
> and you shall answer me. (Job 38:2–3)

This has to have been the most shocking response Job could have expected from God. Anyone I have ever known, when asked the question on the problem of pain, begins to philosophize in his or her own answer. We are all chronically bent toward offering our own solutions. God, in a most surprising move, began to question Job. In fact, He raised about sixty-four questions to Job, one after the other, and compelled Job to open up his own modest stock of certainties.

> Where were you when I laid the earth's foundation?
> Tell me, if you understand.
> Who marked off its dimensions? Surely you know! . . .
> Have you journeyed to the springs of the sea
> or walked in the recesses of the deep?

Have the gates of death been shown to you? . . .
What is the way to the abode of the light?
  And where does darkness reside? . . .
Can you bring forth the constellations in their seasons . . .?
Who endowed the heart with wisdom
  or gave understanding to the mind? . . .
Do you know when the mountain goats give birth?
  Do you watch when the doe bears her fawn?
  (Job 38:4–5, 16–17, 19, 32, 36; 39:1)

So ran the myriad questions, leaving Job completely speechless. He had built his whole argument on the fact that he needed to know what was going on, because only on the basis of that knowledge could his confusion be dissipated. God reminded him, as a first step and only that, that there were a thousand and one things he did not fully understand but had just taken for granted.

Children learn this vital first step early. Have you ever noticed that in every fairy tale there is a condition? "If you do not come back by such and such, you will become a such and such." But beyond that, notice that the person never asks the fairy godmother, "How come?" Because the fairy godmother could legitimately respond, "If that is the way you want it, then tell me, how come there is a fairy land?"[7]

The immensity and specificity of the universe must humble us in the best sense of the word. The more a person knows, the more humble he or she needs to be because the entailments of knowledge remind us constantly of the vastness and intricacy of ultimate reality: the birth of a baby, the nursing of that child at its mother's breast, the boundlessness of a mother's love, the wonder of growth to maturity, the fascinating intricacy of the brain, the enchantment of human sexuality.

A powerful story is told by G. K. Chesterton, called "The Magician." It is the parable of a magician who visited a town and was performing a number of tricks to entertain the crowd. While everyone else was thoroughly enjoying his performance a young scholar sitting near the front of the auditorium persisted in finding his own explanation for every trick. The magician was getting rather exasperated and finally came upon a trick that this intellectual would find unexplainable.

He called the analyst over and asked him, "What color was the light outside your home when you left?"

The scholar answered that it was a red light. "Run along home," said the magician, "and even as you are running I will turn it into a green light."

"You cannot do that!" retorted the young man.

"Oh, yes I can, and I will," came the answer.

The young man began to run toward his house, and as he came within a few feet of it he saw the light change color. Completely astounded, he turned around and ran back to the magician. "All right, how did you do it?"

The magician looked at him and said, "I just sent a couple of angels to change the bulb."

"That is nonsense," came the answer. "Tell me how you did it." No matter how belligerently the scholar protested, he received the same answer: "I sent a couple of angels to change the bulb."

The young man retreated to his science laboratory, trying to figure out how a red light can be changed into a green light. He became so obsessed with his quest that he finally went insane. His sisters came to the magician and implored him to give his trick away just this once so that their brother would regain his sanity.

"But I have already told him the truth," he said.

"All right, then, why don't you tell him something that is not true but sounds reasonable? At least it will bring his sanity back."

The magician reluctantly agreed and fabricated an explanation for his trick, which the young man readily accepted. Immediately he regained his sanity.

Chesterton made the chilling observation that in actuality the critic was more sane when he had no explanation for the red light turning into green. When he bought into the lie that he believed to be a suitable explanation, he was, in fact, truly insane. The application for our time should be evident.[8]

Years ago when I was speaking in a village in Vietnam the audience was principally comprised of poor people, many of them illiterate. I shared with them a story we often told in India, the story of a man who was sitting under a tree that was laden with nuts. He looked up into the tree and mockingly said to God, "Somehow I do not think You are very smart. You have made a huge tree to hold small nuts and a small plant to hold big watermelons. Big tree, small nuts; small plant, big watermelons. Your sense of proportion does not seem to have much meaning." Just then a small nut fell from the tree and hit him on his head. He paused and muttered, "Thank God that was not a watermelon!"

To hear the roar of laughter that erupted and to see the way they enthusiastically jostled one another, as if to congratulate themselves for being so right in their simplicity, was truly delightful. This is not intended to disparage or in any way to mock education and glorify ignorance; it is only intended to dent the inordinate pride that arrogates to itself a strident self-confidence based on the illusion of omniscience. Does this all mean that the intellect has no pursuit in understanding the greatness of the universe? Of course not. It only cautions us to retain the wonder and to remember our finitude. God says, in essence, "Do not assume that you only accept that which you comprehensively understand." He clearly implies that He had given sufficient evidence of His power and design in creation. To seek comprehensive knowledge as the only grounds for belief is unreasonable. There is a world of difference between the words *sufficient* and *comprehensive.* Unless we know that difference we will always wallow in a no-man's land straddling between divinity and finitude.

Francis Schaeffer used to give a very fair illustration on this subject. Suppose you left your home in the morning with two glasses on your table, glass A with two ounces of water in it and glass B, empty. When you returned home at night you noticed that glass B now had water in it and glass A was empty. Further, when you measured the water in glass B, you noticed that there was four ounces of water in it, not two. You might deduce that someone took the water from A and put it into B. But you could also be sure that all of the water did not come from

A, because A only had two ounces of water to start with. The two extra ounces would need a different explanation.

Science may explain "two ounces of this universe," but there is much else that is not within the purview of science. Noted scholars such as Michael Polanyi, one of this century's finest philosophers of science, has cautioned those in the sciences not to lose sight of their own unscientific presuppositions.[9] God challenged Job to admit his limitation and to allow God to be God. God insists that those limitations do and must exist.

But God takes Job beyond just making him think it was all too vast for him. What God wanted him to realize was that this same God who brought such pattern and beauty into a world He had fashioned out of nothing could also bring a pattern and beauty out of Job's brokenness. The universe is both complex and intelligible, and Job was reminded of that.[10] There is intelligence behind the design, as there is also intelligence in helping us cope with suffering.

Think for a moment of the opposite scenario in a Godless universe. To strip this universe of an intelligent first cause leaves us with a mindless force behind everything. I cannot think of worse news for humanity. I am intrigued by the credulity of those who seem to think that proving the accidental arrival of life in this universe will spell victory for the skeptic. One may as well tell a young man, "You are really not the child we had intended to have, but now that you are here, let's make the best of it." I would not want to be on the receiving end of that little speech. That is why God's first approach to Job was to remind him there was a mind and a power infinitely greater than his listening to him. He was not just speaking into a void.

Revealing the Comfort

After leaving Job to ponder the fact that God is both Creator and Designer, God came to Job as Revealer and Comforter. And Job's humbled response was to say, "My ears had heard of you but now my eyes have seen you. Therefore I despise myself and repent in dust and ashes" (Job 42:5–6). The God to whom he had cried out came to meet him as Revealer and Comforter.

There is a place for knowing and hearing and reading. But there has to come a moment of personal surrender. Our commitment to God has sufficient objective truth so that the truth claims can be verified. The Bible is not a fanciful book of spiritual speculation conjured up by dreamers. There are historical, geographical, and philosophical assertions that can be measured and confirmed by the historian, the archeologist, and the philosopher, respectively. But the point of real contact comes when that third-person knowledge—that knowledge *about* God—becomes a first-person trust in God and commitment to His will. Only then does the personal understanding bring a transformed attitude.

The early Israelites made a colossal blunder. Rather than accept spiritual responsibility and come to God directly, they wanted Moses to represent them before God. They asked for a king to deliver them from political responsibility when God had said He desired to be their king. In short, they wanted no direct contact with God.

Church history is littered with the debris of would-be mediators who robbed the common person of the privilege of coming to God directly. The damage inflicted upon humanity and upon Christendom has been incalculable. But it is not just the ebb and flow of history, it is also an assumption that many make that God is unknowable or too distant. The Scriptures remind us that God has graciously invited us to come to Him on a personal level. He reaches out to every man, woman, and child and says, "Come to me, all you who are weary and burdened, and I will give you rest" (Matt. 11:28).

I very seldom like to mention the turning point of my own life, for it is a very private matter and sometimes still hurts to think of it, to say nothing of the embarrassment it must bring my family. But I cannot resist thinking of that most poignant moment of my past. I was seventeen years old when, with neither great intensity or great anguish, I came to the recognition that life had very little meaning. The more I pondered its harsh implication the closer I drew to a decision. That decision was to choose the way of suicide.

I found myself after that attempt lying in a hospital bed, having expelled all the poison that I had taken but unsure if I would recover. There on that bed, with a dehydrated body, the Scriptures were read to me. The flooding of my heart with the news that Jesus Christ could come into my life and that I could know God personally defies the depths to which the truth overwhelmed me. In that moment with a simple prayer of trust, the change from a desperate heart to one that found the fullness of meaning became a reality for me.

God reached down to a teenager in a hospital bed in the city of New Delhi, a mega-city of teeming millions. Imagine! God cared enough to hear my cry. How incredible, that He has a personal interest in the struggles of our lives. I cannot express it better than to say that His self-sufficiency and greatness do not deny us the wonderful joy of being affirmed in our individuality and of knowing that we are of unique value to Him. That was the point of the parable Jesus told about the shepherd who left the ninety-nine sheep in the fold and went looking for the one.

The breadth of the gospel in its implications for history and for all of humanity ought never to diminish the application that is personal. It had to come as a revelation to Job that much of his knowledge of God had come through the thoughts of other people—thoughts never personally pursued. That is precisely the predicament his friends were in, rich in allusions to what others had said but impoverished in their own personal knowledge of God.

It was to that same glaring weakness in the apostle Peter's life that Jesus directed His attention. Peter gladly quoted what others said of Jesus. But Jesus asked him, "Who do *you* say I am?" (Mark 8:29, emphasis added). This is why no one speaks with such authority of the devastation of sin as the one who has experienced it. No one knows the restoring power of God like the one who has walked that road. "My ears had heard of you, but now my eyes have seen you." God is not just the God of power in creation; He is the God of presence in our affliction. He had not abandoned Job but was with him personally.

Until pain is seen in a personal context and its solution is personally felt, every other solution, however good, will seem academic. All the answers that one might offer to a hurting person will fall on deaf ears until that person has come to a personal recognition that God has spoken and revealed Himself in His Word first and then in his or her own experience.

A Counterperspective

Having reached that point, a new discovery came into focus for Job. He had earlier asked, "If a man dies, will he live again?" He was now able to answer his own question with firm assurance:

> I know that my Redeemer lives,
> and that in the end he will stand upon the earth.
> And after my skin has been destroyed,
> yet in my flesh I will see God;
> I myself will see him
> with my own eyes—I, and not another.
> How my heart yearns within me! (Job 19:25–27)

All suffering has to be dealt with personally but also with a real understanding that there is life beyond the grave. Just think of Job's confidence: "After my skin has been destroyed, yet in my flesh I will see God." There is a perspective from God's side that those of us locked in a temporal frame of reference can never see. Death was not going to break Job's communion with God. The songwriter said it: "Let me see this world, dear Lord, as though I were looking through Your eyes."[11]

When the prophet Habakkuk was struggling with all the violence he saw around him, he asked God to explain it to him. He ended by saying, "He makes my feet like the feet of a deer, he enables me to go on the heights." For the first time he saw human suffering from a vantage point he had never seen before, from God's perspective (Hab. 3:17–19).

Having suffered much in his own life, the eminent and afflicted poet William Cowper expressed it beautifully:

Blind unbelief is sure to err,
And scan His works in vain;
God is His own interpreter,
And He will make it plain.[12]

Job was being taken one step at a time—from recognizing the Creator and Designer to meeting Him as Revealer and Comforter and finally to knowing Him as Mediator and Savior. This beautiful truth could only be understood by Job in a very limited fashion. Those of us who look back to the cross have a much fuller understanding of the grand connotation the word *Savior* has. Little did Job know that a day would come when the purest one of all, in whom there was no sin, would suffer and die that we who lived in sin might find His rest and purity.

A very moving story is told about a renowned preacher who lost his young wife. In the confusion of her fresh grief, his little daughter came to him and asked why it was that if Jesus has died for our sins we still have to die. He waited for the appropriate illustration with which to help her young mind understand what God has done for us. On the way to the funeral, their car was behind a big truck. Drawing her attention to the truck, he looked at his daughter and asked if she had to be run over, would she rather be run over by a truck or by its shadow on the side of the road.

"Why of course," she said, "the shadow would be better, because it would not hurt as much."

He paused and answered her gently, "That is what Jesus has done for you. On His death upon the cross, He let the truck of God's judgment pass over Him. Only the shadow of death goes over us now."

By taking our place upon the cross and bridging the chasm between God, who offered life, and humanity, which deserved death, Christ spanned the greatest gulf. Our thirst for a mediator before God is a very genuine cry that has been expressed in virtually every theistic religion. But for most, the God who is out there is treated as still being out there. For others, the quest to bring God near without humanizing Him has been a particular struggle. Thus in Greek mythology, heroes and the personification of ideals proliferate. In pantheism, avatars, or incarnations, form the bulk of revelation. But in the Christian faith, the fact that God comes close while remaining transcendent is very unique. To what degree Job understood this will always remain moot, but that he cried out even in his primitive understanding of redemption that a Savior would understand his suffering, plead His cause, and vindicate him is remarkable.

In short, this discovery affirmed one of Job's convictions but shattered one aspect of his theology. Job had repeatedly said that as far as he knew he had lived an honorable life. But he had assumed all along that if one walked the straight and narrow and lived a life of purity, prosperity and freedom from pain would naturally follow. This was a false conclusion.

Over the years of history we have seen this unfortunate deduction made time and again. We may even recall that when John the Baptist was put into prison he wondered if Jesus was indeed who He claimed to be. The implication was, "If He is the Messiah, then why am I in prison?" The apostle Peter could not for a moment conceive of the Son of God going to a cross. As hard as it is to accept, suffering is not always because of one's personal sin, but suffering will always have to be dealt with personally. Our Lord Himself bore the pain of that which was not His own doing, but the Captain of our salvation was made perfect, that is, complete, through suffering. Life must never be viewed from the isolated instances of one's personal struggle. There is a big picture and a complete picture into which our personal struggle fits. That picture is in the mind of God. The closer we draw to Him the clearer that picture becomes. And part of that picture is pain and desolation.

But if Job had his theology shattered and if the picture told him that even the righteous could suffer pain and hurt, what was the one thing he would need to know more than anything else? That is where we find the answer that Job needed most, as much as we do when walking through deep waters. I can best answer this by an illustration.

Some years ago while I had the privilege of speaking at Moody

Bible Institute we had the extraordinary blessing of listening to a talk by Professor Charles Cooper, who taught there. He sat in a chair as he told his story that was still so fresh in his memory and in the memories of those who knew him. He spoke of the thrill he'd felt of being newly married and of the delight of a young love. Yet only four months into his marriage, tragedy struck.

His wife was returning from a trip, and he and his mother-in-law went to the airport to pick her up. As the plane pulled up to the jetway, they saw ambulances and police cars closing in on the back of the aircraft and personnel from those vehicles running up the back stairway. But Charles's focus was on the front of the plane from where his wife would disembark. All of a sudden, his mother-in-law clasped his arm and pointed to a stretcher that was being removed from the back door of the airplane. On the stretcher was obviously a body, covered by a white sheet. But that was not all. Hanging from the stretcher was a purse that they recognized as his wife's.

A few moments later their names were called over the loudspeaker and in shock, they were informed that shortly before landing, without any previous history of such a condition, his young wife had suffered a fatal heart attack.

How does one respond to news so debilitating? Charles Cooper walked us through his own journey of pain. His closing comment will forever ring in my ears. He said that the cards, the letters, the phone calls, the embraces, and the love of friends all played a part in helping him to survive. "But what kept me going more than anything else was my confidence in the character of God." That was the bottom line.

This is the adjustment Job needed. Constantly focusing on his own character and purity, he had lost sight of the character of God Himself. Those who have walked this path hold on to that truth with all the strength they have. God is not only all-powerful. He is perfect in goodness. We must trust Him even when the times are grim.

At the end, Job discovered that this God who was his Creator and Designer, his Revealer and Comforter, his Mediator and Savior, was also his Strengthener and Restorer.

THE TRIUMPHAL MOMENT

There is intrigue and experience beyond anything we might have expected as a closure to this Book of Job. Job was now fully cognizant of the fact that the whole problem of suffering was indeed beyond his comprehension and that his knowledge of God as Creator, Revealer, Savior, and Restorer was sufficient to see him through what he did not know. Beyond that, however, was the greatest surprise of all.

Job's friends were severely reprimanded by God for the part they had played, and they had to come to Job, not only for forgiveness, but to ask him to mediate on their behalf to receive God's forgiveness. In other words, he who had pled for a mediator in his own quandary became a mediator himself to bridge the chasm between his erudite friends and God.

The Bible says of our Lord that having suffered Himself, Jesus is now able to intercede on our behalf. In a small sense, Job was given a glimpse of the heart of God by representing his friends before God. Just as Jesus Himself, having been betrayed by His own, stood in a place of intercession for them, and just as Joseph, betrayed by his brothers, stood in a position of forgiving and restoring them, so now Job interceded for his friends. Just as his own Redeemer had brought him close to God, so now he played that role for Eliphaz, Bildad, and Zophar. Talk about a higher perspective and about seeing it from God's view!

THE TRUTHS THAT TRANSFORMED

We can draw numerous conclusions from this enormous struggle that Job went through. First and foremost, we must understand that suffering, death, disease, pain, and bereavement are all part of life, whether we be righteous or unrighteous.

Second, we see that the role of a friend is very pivotal in seeing people through their times of anguish. Let us never underestimate this point. God's answer for burdened, hurting hearts may well be the shoulders of a friend as we bear one another's burdens and so fulfill the law of Christ.

Third, we know that most answers of this nature require a process. The questions must become more selfless before the answer becomes more personal. For Job, as for us, the process was as necessary as the answer. After I spoke recently at a lectureship in Bombay, India, on the subject of God and the problem of pain, a gentleman came to me and spoke of a tragedy in his family. His daughter had been killed in a plane crash a few years ago. He said to me, "I used to think that time was a healer. I no longer believe that. I now believe that time is only the revealer of how God does the healing."

Fourth, we have learned, as Job did, that the answer to suffering is more relational than it is propositional. Those who know God personally and understand the cross are better able to find help in the dark night of the soul than those who merely tackle their problems philosophically. And the man or woman who has suffered much is often a redeemer-like figure to those whose lives are devoid of a close walk with God and whose answers may be only surface deep. A renowned Christian leader once told me, "When you are looking for wisdom, always look for one who has suffered much but whose faith has remained unshaken."

I saw this principle in action a few years ago when I was visiting in Nanjing, China, with a friend. We had the great privilege of spending a couple of hours with one of China's most renowned evangelists, Wang Ming Tau. His was a fascinating story of imprisonment under Mao Zedong's brutal regime.

He had been incarcerated for his faith in Christ, and unable to face a life of permanent imprisonment, he had recanted his faith and been released. But as a free man he knew he had betrayed his Lord. Troubled at his failure, he decided that if life in prison was what God wanted for him, then that was what he would gladly accept. With a renewed commitment to his Lord he walked the streets of Beijing, shouting, "My name is Peter, I have betrayed my Lord! My name is Peter, I have betrayed my Lord!"

As he had expected, he was immediately rearrested. For nineteen more years behind bars he suffered for Christ. When he finished telling us his story, he asked if he could sing us a hymn that he sang in prison every day. His body aged, and his hands all gnarled, with his wife, almost blind, sitting next to him, he sang,

> All the way my Savior leads me—
> What have I to ask beside?
> Can I doubt His tender mercy,
> Who through life has been my guide?
> Heavenly peace, divinest comfort,
> Here by faith in Him to dwell!
> For I know, whate'er befall me,
> Jesus doeth all things well.[13]

As I sat in his small room listening to him sing, I glanced at the three young men who were seated on the floor, their faces lifted to him as he sang. They had come to visit him, and before they left, they asked him to pray for them. There is something so moving about able-bodied young people seeking the prayers of an old, fragile man or woman. But in the most biblical sense of the term they knew the principle of redemptive suffering, wherein one whose own life has been touched by the Savior in his or her own suffering can pray more honestly and effectively on behalf of those who have not yet gone through the fire. I could picture Job smiling with approval.

Four

The Cry of a Guilty Conscience

IN 1969, writer and activist for the cause of Holocaust victims Simon Wiesenthal penned his thought-provoking book, *The Sunflower.* Few writings have captured with such raw emotion and penetrating intellect the agony he personally experienced in one of history's darkest moments. His theme was the unshakable and unexplainable struggle that we as human beings have with guilt. From beginning to end the book was interwoven with this titanic struggle, both in his own thoughts and in the thoughts of other contributors who responded to the author's quest for an answer. In his case the problem only intensified when imprisoned in a concentration camp.

In the story, which is autobiographical, he related how he had been taken from a death camp to a makeshift army hospital. On a day of surprising events, he was ushered by a nurse to the side of a Nazi soldier who had asked to have a few private moments with a Jew. Not knowing what lay ahead of him, Wiesenthal warily entered the room and was brought face to face with a fatally wounded man, bandaged from head to toe. The man turned toward him and spoke in what was little more than a cracked whisper. Almost numbed by the experience and wondering if it was real or imaginary, Wiesenthal nervously endured what was a tense monologue. The soldier unburdened his heart of a heinous crime he had committed when he set ablaze an entire village of Jews. He was unable to silence from his memory the screams of those men, women, and children as they burned to death at his whim.

What, then, was his reason for beckoning this stranger to his bedside? Knowing that he himself was dying, he was making a last desperate effort to seek forgiveness from one whose people he had killed. As the man pleaded with him, Wiesenthal could not bring himself to pronounce such forgiveness. In fact, during the confession, Wiesenthal made numerous efforts to leave but was implored by the officer to "please stay." He needed to get this off his heart. But the struggle was equally intense on the other side. How can I, thought Wiesenthal, by a mere pronouncement or the wave of my hand just absolve anyone of so monumental a crime against humanity? At the hands of the Nazis he had himself lost eighty-nine of his own relatives.

If that were all this book were about, the theme would be arresting enough. But years later the author wondered if he had done the right thing. Should not he really have set the man's heart at ease by accepting his death-bed repentance and by offering the forgiveness he so earnestly sought? As a result of his own soul-searching, Wiesenthal wrote to thirty-two men and women of high regard—scholars, social theorists, psychologists, and others. Twenty-six of the thirty-two affirmed his choice not to offer the forgiveness that was sought. Their reasons varied from doubting his individual right to forgive a crime committed against a whole race to understanding and identifying with his reluctance to forgive deeds so ghastly. But six suggested that he should have taken the high road here and given pardon, for his part at least.

What a vortex of human emotion swirls around this subject of guilt! We come up against it in our families. We battle for it in our courtrooms. We philosophize about it in the classroom. We try to explain it with psychology. We shout about it from the pulpit. We wrestle with it in private. So pervasive and deep-seated are its ramifications that some in professional counseling have gone so far as to say that guilt is the cornerstone of all neuroses.[1]

Even those not well acquainted with the writings of William Shakespeare are familiar with those rueful cries of Lady Macbeth. In the story, Macbeth was spurred on by his wife to murder King Duncan and seize the throne. After the murder it was she who took the blood of the king and smeared it on the sleeping guards to implicate them in the murder. But the plot focuses later on Lady Macbeth herself, walking in her sleep, night after night. Staring at her hands she pleads, "Out, damned spot! Out, I say! One; two. . . . Here's the smell of the blood still. All the perfumes of Arabia will not sweeten this little hand. Oh, oh, oh!"[2]

Observing her pitiful plight, the doctor says, "This disease is beyond my practice."

How concretely expressive is the word *disease* when it carries its underlying meaning—dis-ease—which speaks of the connection between the spirit and the body, the suffering of one who is no longer at ease in the flesh because of the torment of the soul. That is the pathology of guilt. It may well have been with Lady Macbeth in mind that Lord Byron said, "Oh that pang, where more than madness lies, The worm that will not sleep and never dies."[3]

Guilt is, in fact, one of the oldest sentiments ever expressed in writing, dealt with in the earliest verses of the Bible. After the familiar narrative of the temptation in Genesis 3, we read of Adam and Eve hiding from God's beckoning voice calling, "Where are you?" The question was intended to highlight not so much a place as a condition. Neither Adam nor Eve could break free from the ensuing anguish of a choice made in willful violation of God's command.

In similar manner, in Psalm 51 David spoke of the pain within him when his adultery with Bathsheba and the murder of her husband was brought to light. He likened it to the agony of a person with broken bones. And who can forget the image conjured up by Pontius Pilate trying to wash his hands of the guilt that he feared from having sent Jesus to the cross? Even today there is a mountain named after him in

Switzerland, Mount Pilatus, and legend says that every so often his ghost is seen coming to the waters of Lucerne to wash away his guilt. Whether it is likened to a ghost that haunts, to a wounded spirit, or to a fractured body, all cultures and religions wrestle with the issue of guilt.

Such a universal feeling has compelled every human being either to deal with such conflict or to find a convincing way to explain it away. It is a theme that captivates readers. Many great novelists have tackled it and filled page after page with the ways and means by which the human mind has sought to cope with guilt. Raskolnikov in Dostoevsky's *Crime and Punishment* is a classic example. After analyzing the tricks to which some have resorted or the candor with which others have faced up to their guilt, some very definite but clearly limited options emerge. There are at least six different responses that humanity has made toward our battle with guilt.

EXPEL GUILT BY IRREVERENCE

The first response one may have, and many fall into this attitude toward guilt, is to expel any and all personal guilt with a brazen irreverence. This posture toward guilt daringly implies that nothing in life is essentially sacred and that guilt is a conditioned response orchestrated principally by religion. Since religion, they argue, is a hangover from pre-modern times and nothing falls into an actual category of right and wrong, guilt should be erased from our society's lexicon and jeered out of existence.

Just as the pre-modern pagan prostituted religion and enslaved himself or herself to chains of vain repetitions, so the modern materialist castrates religion and struts about with a vanity that is to be equally pitied. This arrogant response has gained much popularity and has licensed the wholesale ridicule of things that were once held to be sacred. The symptoms of this are often evidenced in seemingly innocuous situations but are ultimately carried into the deadliest forms of hatred and violence. Watch the average television program and see the jocular sentiments conferred upon illegitimacy, adultery, profanity, and a host of other lifestyles that ought to have merited some caution. The media's mockery vented upon then Vice President Dan Quayle when he voiced concern over a popular sitcom that so thoughtlessly and frivolously celebrated unwed motherhood underscores how abusive this irreverent attitude can be—almost to a point of ruining the life of its critics. The unabated outrage of the entertainment personalities who ridiculed and trashed Quayle's comments spoke volumes for our time. It was accepted that the glamorous people whose lives espoused nothing sacred should be hailed as heroes and heroines while the person in high office who called for decency should be branded a fool.

Perhaps one could accept this trivializing of life and its options if we were all approving of it, or even if those who prided themselves in it were to be consistent. But this kind of belittling is a subtle form of attack, and the mockers do not play by their own rules when the tables are turned and something they regard as sacred is vilified.

Far too much damage is done to our emotional and spiritual well-being when we deal irresponsibly with matters that to many are sacred. Our irreverence, therefore, is costly when it meets up with the sharp edges of reality. At some point guilt must be acknowledged, or else the irreverent will end up victimizing themselves.

History's Grim Reminder

In the closing years of this century the quintessential questions raised by millions on the subject of guilt have invariably been built around the Second World War and the atrocities of the Holocaust. This is not without reason, both because it is still fresh in the memory of many and also because of the magnitude of the criminality. I shall therefore relate two illustrations from within that context, one from fact and the other from fiction, which show how damning the impact of irreverence can be when guilt is dismissed either in reality or in imagination.

In 1960 the Israeli Mossad masterminded one of the most incredible feats of its history when it tracked down Adolf Eichmann in his hideaway home in Argentina. From beginning to end the plot bore all the marks of a sophisticated made-for-the-movies script. The point man implementing the whole plan was Peter Malkin. Several of Malkin's family members had died at the hands of the Third Reich and he, therefore, had personal passion to contribute to this effort. In particular, he still grieved over the loss of his sister and his six-year-old nephew, Peter.

As Malkin closed in on the capture, he covertly monitored the comings and goings of Adolf Eichmann in his home and noticed a regular routine. Every day when Eichmann came home from work he was excitedly greeted by a young boy who threw his arms up in the air and welcomed him. Malkin would often think of his own little nephew when he saw this affectionate reception night after night from the little boy. He was taken, as well, by Eichmann's tender response, having only thought of him as one of the cold-hearted architects of human extermination.

Finally one day, the plans meticulously laid, Malkin crept up behind Eichmann as he was on his way from the bus stop to his home, and with three simple words—"Un momentito, Señor"—he caused Eichmann to turn around and he captured him. With lightning speed Eichmann was dragged into a waiting car. The words simply asked for "One moment, Sir," but carried the weight of the eternal and ineradicable cry from the heart of one representing millions—that a murderous life be brought to justice. The rest of the story is now history, having led to the trial and execution of the man whose name had signified terror to multitudes and under whose watch tens of thousands were sent to the gas chambers.

But one private moment between Malkin and Eichmann may have spelled the greatest blow to Malkin himself, leaving him more heartbroken than ever. Unable to keep that conversation to himself any longer, Malkin finally broke his silence after thirty years to write about it recently. It was of supreme importance to Malkin that Eichmann voice two things. First, he wanted desperately to know, *How?* How was it possible that an ordinary human being could orchestrate such untold evil and feel no guilt about it? What prompted such unparalleled brutality?

But there was a second thing—a very personal and nagging question. Malkin had found out that the little boy who so enthralled Eichmann was his own six-year-old son, born to him in Argentina. Malkin thought he had all the emotional weight needed to pose the question and raised it at the most opportune moment when Eichmann spoke passionately of how he missed his son.

"My sister's boy, my favorite playmate—he was just your son's age . . . also blond and blue-eyed, just like your son. And you killed him." He waited for an explanation, confident that Eichmann could make the extension and feel with Malkin the way he felt about his nephew.

Eichmann paused and then with complete indifference muttered, "But your nephew was Jewish, wasn't he?"

Mustering every ounce of self-restraint he possessed, Malkin walked out of the room and, in his own words, "sobbed uncontrollably." He was speechless for a long time.[4]

A precious life had been trivialized and the trivialization callously justified. Hate wore a face of such tranquillity that it was terrifying. The sacredness of a person's birth and ethnicity were remorselessly violated and the sanctity of life irreverently profaned.

Assuming the intrinsic worth of our fellow human beings is at the heart of all existence. One's life and place of birth are inheritances not conferred by some collective agreement. They are personal and inviolable. Life at its core is sacred and dependent, and there is only one who can claim the power for giving it—God. If then life itself is sacred, both in its essence and in its trust, how can it be lived or abused as if it were valueless?

I have often wondered what went into Eichmann's mind as he said those words. What moral input was he giving to himself to legitimize his actions? Was there something a person's race connoted to him that made a man or woman dispensable? These are painful questions that cannot be left unaddressed. I believe this question here has much to say about the nature of guilt, because Eichmann's answer cannot be justified without addressing the larger question of either the intrinsic sanctity of life or the outright worthlessness to all that we do. Was

Eichmann saying more than we would dare to hear? Let me attempt an answer.

Truth by Way of Fiction

The second illustration, by way of the arts, gives us a clue to what may have been behind such horrifying indifference. The pertinence of the theme of guilt becomes quite overwhelming as we unwrap this question. Novelists have a way of dealing with reality by fictionalizing the characters into whose mouths they place life's most undeniable sentiments. I borrow from George Steiner's book *The Portage to San Christabel of A.H.*, the A.H. standing for Adolf Hitler. The story is undoubtedly filled with imagination, but there is a reason for it. The basic plot is that Adolf Hitler did not die as history tells us but instead fled to the swamps of South America to hide.

Against all odds his pursuers tracked him down and brought him back to trial. The obvious question was put to him, too. Why the death sentence especially leveled on one particular race? He gave three reasons, the final one being that "there had to be a final solution." By that he meant that there had to be a total extermination. Was there a reason he crafted that final solution? Could it have been something deeper, possibly a veiled but concerted plan at eradication of the supernatural?

We do know from the study of philosophy that Hitler was profoundly influenced by Nietzsche. For Nietzsche, religion had weakened human dignity and power by foisting upon people the notions of guilt and repentance. These were utterly dehumanizing and inhibiting to societal progress and to human power, he said. Could it be, then, that the people through whom the moral law came were the ones who were to blame for the curse of guilt? Such weakness had to be dealt a death blow! Was that a driving force behind Hitler's determination to do away with them?

Even if that is not granted, we must recognize that in our own time it is repeatedly stated by some hostile to the Christian faith that religion is a crutch and a barrier to progress. Voices are heard, articles are written, and movies are made that take full aim at the "crippling role of religion" in human progress. Any espousal of morality is debunked. Life, it is assumed, is not conferred by God. Let us remove the Ten Commandments from the school walls. If there are no commandments there will be no such thing as guilt. If there is no such thing as guilt, then by all means, let us humiliate and marginalize those whose voices bring guilt to society—and a different kind of a "final solution" is under way.

I was startled at a meeting in Washington to hear one Jewish journalist make the comment that he thought Christians would be the Jews of the twenty-first century. Why did he think so? Because there is little doubt that no other major religious voice in this world cries out for people to deal with sin, to repent, and to come to God for forgiveness. Hate and anger vented against the Christian gains momentum when a society wants to live life without restraint.

Unlivable on Its Own Terms

But this is the very society that arrogates to itself a moral right to self-determination. On what basis is a moral right claimed when notions of morality are dismissed as oppressive and stultifying? When we look back upon the horror of Hitler's final solution, every civilized voice cries out against such desacralizing of life, and the nations victimized brought the perpetrators to justice. But an Eichmannesque irreverence knows no restraint and tolerates no condemnation. The world in turn was shocked when, like Eichmann, most of the accused denied any guilt. In short, the collective conscience of humanity, though it chooses to live autonomously, that is, by a self-law, nevertheless affirms that the expulsion of guilt by irreverence is repugnant and makes life plainly unlivable.

To expel the moral law may seem very cavalier and liberating, but the ramifications are catastrophic. Irreverence is just another word for self-worship and the destruction of all that stands in its way. The killing of Abel by Cain was such an effort. Abel symbolized acceptance before God; Cain, rejection. Cain's final solution was to silence the voice of the one whose life reflected sanctity.

Similarly, Joseph represented the special favor of God. His brothers' final solution was to do away with him. John the Baptizer portended to Herod a judgment that was inevitable. Herod's final solution was to decapitate him. Elijah warned Jezebel of history's warning when decency is mocked. Jezebel's final solution was to pursue him until he wanted to die. Jesus represented the voice of God to a corrupt priesthood and to power-mongering political authorities. Their final solution was to send Him to the cross.

To silence the voice that reminds us of our guilt is always the "final solution." The past is littered with the debris of irreverence. In a final sense, therefore, it was not so much Jewishness that may have been behind Eichmann's slaughter. He certainly denied it himself. Racism and ethnic hostility may be the poison tip of the arrow that rips away at societal existence. But what carries the arrow is hatred in general and a passion in the heart to play God and obliterate anything that hints at a moral law over us. That is why the profane celebrate the fall of a professed moralist—because it levels the playing field and stabs at the heart of morality, rendering in their eyes all moral talk as hypocritical.

But even the irreverent find it impossible to live without denunciation. And all denunciation implies a moral doctrine of some kind. They speak in anger against those who call for moral reasoning. But they are even angrier when they are on the wrong end of someone's immorality or when they come up on the receiving end of injustice. Put simply, guilt does not disappear by attempting to silence God. The logic of it makes life unlivable. The final solution turns painfully inward.

SMOTHER GUILT BY PRIDE

There is a second option we have, and that is to somehow suppress any and all intimations of guilt under the weight of our own egos. Guilt can be smothered by pride. How we are perceived in public or esteemed by our circle of friends is for most people an all-consuming passion. It has led countless men and women, when confronted with wrongdoing, to scamper for cover under a flurry of excuses. Listen carefully to the rationalizing and the explanations when a person is charged with having violated a law or is exposed for unsavory behavior. Observe the mind then in its most sinister maneuvers. Self-exoneration is the genius of reason in its bent toward irrationality. There is no limit to which the mind will not stoop for cover when wanting to appear justified.

While irreverence applies only to some, this proclivity to look good when under the accusing eye spares nobody. Solomon declared centuries ago that there is nothing new under the sun. When Adam blamed Eve and Eve blamed the serpent it appeared at first blush that the buck stopped there. Evil has an enormous power to seduce. But the greater tragedy ensues when the one so seduced refuses to accept any blame. Like most of life's basic lessons, this one is reinforced time and again; yet, many never recognize the stumbling block of pride in themselves but hate it when they see it in others.

One of the most classic examples comes to us from the life of King Saul in the Old Testament. When the story began it was with all the hope and promise of a humble man who had been suddenly and surprisingly anointed king of Israel. He was to be their first monarch, and Samuel met him to break the good news to him. Saul's response was admirable. When Samuel said, "And to whom is all the desire of Israel turned, if not to you and all your father's family?" Saul spoke from the overflow of his heart and protested. "But am I not a Benjamite, from the smallest tribe of Israel, and is not my clan the least of all the clans of the tribe of Benjamin? Why do you say such a thing to me?" (1 Sam. 9:20–21).

Here was a man toward whom the nation and God Himself reached, but here was a man who saw nothing in himself to make him worthy of such privilege. Yet the brief enjoyment of power left its deadly aftertaste and poisoned his mind into believing that he was indeed due that greatness and acclaim. Shortly after his accession to the throne he willfully and wantonly disobeyed God. Samuel was left with no choice but to confront him. Saul tried every trick in the book in feigning innocence, but the evidence of his disobedience was irrefutable. Finally there emerged two obvious clues to what had happened to this man.

First, when Samuel went to meet him he was told that Saul had gone to build a monument in his own honor. A change from honest humility to blatant self-aggrandizement may at first appear as only a fleeting thing or even a fickle disposition. But the depths of this entrapment are like thorns of steel in the flesh of ambition.

As time went by, David, Saul's would-be successor, won his victory over Goliath, Israel's most feared enemy. The Bible tells us that the women came out from all the towns of Israel to meet King Saul with singing and dancing. And as they danced they sang, "Saul has slain his thousands, and David his tens of thousands." Then comes this telling description. "Saul was very angry; this refrain galled him. . . . And from that time on Saul kept a jealous eye on David" (1 Sam. 18:6–9). No dream is as sure of being doomed as that which makes being number one life's supreme pursuit.

When confronted by Samuel, Saul scurried for cover under a blanket of reasons, pleading, in effect, "I have played the fool!" (see 1 Sam. 15:24). But Saul had done much more than just play the fool. He refused to admit to his addiction to pride, which was the source of his destruction. Benjamin Franklin's words, "Pride breakfasted with plenty, dined with poverty, and supped with infamy,"[5] are most appropriate for Saul's epitaph.

How many millions in this world will never enjoy a walk with God because of individual pride that makes them unable to acknowledge their guilt before Him.

To strut into a courtroom guilty and claim innocence is not power but weakness.

To refuse to acknowledge failure is not success but self-deception.

To resist repentance before God is not intelligence but folly.

To be puffed up with pride in the face of wrongdoing is not to become bigger but to become hollow.

Alexander Pope summed it up in the following way:

> Of all the causes which conspire to blind
> Man's erring judgment, and misguide the mind,
> What the weak head with strongest bias rules,
> Is pride, the never-failing vice of fools.[6]

The resistance to being ordinary or to admitting to failure is understandable. Which of us likes to face up to our weaknesses? But pride spawns every other vice and is, therefore, the most destructive of all offenses. C. S. Lewis said it well:

> You may remember, when I was talking about sexual immorality, I warned you that the center of Christian morals did not lie there. Well now we have come to the center. . . . The utmost evil, is Pride. Unchastity, anger, greed, drunkenness, and all that, are mere fleabites in comparison. It was through Pride that the devil became the devil. Pride leads to every other vice: it is the complete anti-God state of mind.[7]

This truism may have been the reason why, in each of the first two temptations that Satan placed before Jesus, appealing to His pride was an essential element. In the first, it was to "change the stones to bread, and the world will follow you." In the second, "jump and see if the angels will protect you" (see Luke 4:3, 9–10).

The subtle shift in Satan's appeal shows that even pride has stages. The one who seeks an immediate excuse for his or her pride or seeks the approval of others reveals a vestige of embarrassment or need so that he or she may "look good." Uncorrected, that degenerates to a stage where that need is thrown aside. Peter Kreeft said succinctly, "Pride is not pleasure in being praised, wanting to please others. . . . That too shows humility. The exemplars of pride are not movie stars but dictators."[8]

This extremely important point is easily missed. The lowest point of pride is reached when an excuse to explain a choice is not even sought because the choice itself is deemed sufficient explanation for any action. "My right," we read, writ large, a dozen times a day. Such a person has placed himself or herself beyond reach. It is for this very reason that God goes to great lengths to keep us from that kind of pride which becomes demagogic and which insulates us from the reasoning voice of another. Most of us have lived through ordeals where we have seen this happen to somebody but often ignore that we are all susceptible to it. When a point of not caring for any other person's counsel or warning has been reached, when we bask in our own success, thinking ourselves invincible, then God might need to take drastic measures to break that stranglehold upon us.

Centuries ago Thomas Aquinas carried the danger of this kind of pride to a rather startling conclusion and made his point in a provocative way.

> In order to overcome pride, God punishes certain men by allowing them to fall into sins of the flesh which though they be less grievous are more evidently shameful. . . . From this indeed, the gravity of pride is made manifest. For just as a wise physician in order to cure a worse disease allows the patient to contract one that is less dangerous, so the sin of pride is shown to be more grievous by the very fact that as a remedy, God allows men to fall into other sins.[9]

Though this may seem extreme and hard to believe, listen to the words of Richard Dortch, the president of PTL following the pitiful scandal that brought down that ministry and marked a turning point in the attitudes of people all over the world toward those in ministry: "It took the tragedy, the kick in the teeth, to bring us to our senses."[10] He went on to talk of the blinding power of the camera that turns ordinary people into potentates—within minutes. "Cars wait for you. . . . You get to go to the front of the line. . . . It all made us less than what we were meant to be," he said.

Jesus saved His strongest words for those who thought themselves strong and His gentlest words for those who saw themselves as weak. He consistently reminded His audience that the glory of His kingdom was not shown in the power of individual attainments but in the simplicity of a little child's faith.

In short, as the expulsion of guilt by irreverence makes life unlivable, the smothering of guilt by pride makes one's whole life unaccountable.

CONCEAL GUILT BY FEAR

One of the most tormenting ways to deal with guilt is to try to conceal it and live with the fear of exposure. Envy, it has been said, is the only one of the seven deadly sins that does not bring immediate gratification. We may add that fear in the midst of guilt also offers no gratification because it adds apprehension to remorse. Just as a blackmailer is never satisfied or sufficiently compensated, so the one who lives in fear while nursing guilt ends up by blackmailing his or her own heart in order to pay the mind. And the heart is never consoled, for the mind is never sufficiently paid.

A wrong that is concealed seldom stops within the one who harbors that hurt. The pain is sooner or later spread to others, particularly to those closest to us. Victimless crimes are an illusion. The story of Jacob's deception of his father shows us how a multitude, indeed, a nation was wronged as a result. Deceit is a monster that needs constant feeding. In an attempt to steal the blessing, Jacob thought he would only deceive his father and flee to some place of refuge until his father's anger subsided. But his duplicity severely wounded the entire household. Because of his sin he would be absent from his mother's bedside when she died. Esau spent years tracking him down, and when the moment of confrontation between the brothers finally arrived, Jacob wrestled all night in prayer because of his fear that the wrong he had committed years before would be avenged against his children. He could no longer run. The harsh reality is that during thousands of years of history in the Middle East blood has been spilled because of wrongs that were carried forward for generations. To think that deception and cheating can be covered up with impunity is to fly in the face of reality.

The devastating consequences of guilt that is concealed by fear are easy enough to demonstrate. The difficulty is in knowing how best to confront the person without ravaging a life already so plundered. Experience dictates that sensitivity be at the forefront when dealing with one overtaken by fear. At the same time truth demands that such an individual be honestly addressed lest, in a desire not to add to the pain they already feel, we rob them of the possibility of healing. Sometimes such fear may not even be induced by one's personal offense but from being trapped behind a mask or of running from reality.

Many years ago I was speaking before an audience that consisted primarily of junior high and high school students. The challenge was a difficult one for me as I knew full well that what I had to say was no more important than how it was said. No audience is more ready to expose a speaker's failure than an audience of restless teenagers. At the same time no audience is more open to acknowledge its needs than a young audience that has gained confidence in the speaker. After my last session, I let it be known that if anyone had a personal need that he or she needed to talk about I would be available to take a few moments with each one. Within minutes the sign-up sheet was full.

The first student to come, though she made a valiant effort to look calm and composed, sat very nervously and did not do too well at masking a troubled heart. Her entire conversation was about a friend that I shall call Karen. Karen was suicidal, I was told, and in dire need of help. This young woman wanted to know how best to help Karen and keep her from taking her own life. As the minutes ticked away, I interrupted her and asked, "Are you sure you came here to talk about Karen, or is there something more important on your mind?"

There was an annoyed look of surprise on her face, a hard swallow, and then she could conceal her battle no more. Her tears flowed as I had seldom seen, and I felt there was so much bottled up deep within her that I would need both more time and help to bring any comfort to her. But even at that I did not realize how far out of my depth I would be.

As she continued to weep she unfolded a story of sexual molestation by her own father that had begun when she had been seven years old, a wretched hell that had been thrust upon her sporadically for nearly ten years. "I have been terrified of telling anybody because I do not know what this will do to my family and what this will do to my father. Will he end up in jail? Will my mother by able to manage the shock and hurt?"

I knew immediately that her need was greater than my ability. All I could do to conceal my own shock was to be silent for several moments. I shall not protract this story except to say that somehow we were able to immediately bring solace to her situation through professional help. But I could not rid from my mind how close she had come once again, after ten years of being a victim and keeping it within, to concealing the truth for fear of the ramifications. "Karen" became the smokescreen to hide the reality that a life was being systematically dismembered.

Many used this same ploy when they talked to Jesus. They would throw one question after another in order to hide the real struggle beneath them all. Carried to a drastically different level, this same tendency belies all our national preoccupation with one social or economic crisis after another. No one wants to admit that at the heart of our malady is a mangled spirituality. The story from Greek mythology of Aphrodite's infidelities may still have something to say to us. Living as she was in her unfaithfulness, she gave birth to two sons among others, one called Eros and the other called Phobos. Illicit indulgences beget eroticism and fear. This generation has birthed these twin monsters.

If expelling guilt by irreverance makes life unlivable and smothering it by pride makes one's life unaccountable, then concealing guilt by fear makes life unbearable.

DISMISS GUILT AS CULTURAL

The most convenient escape in a confused society is to glibly brush aside guilt as a cultural appendage. Such an academic dismissal of moral reality fails to take into account that even when we differ culturally from one another in our behavior, the reasons that justify that behavior are often the same. In other words, there are some meta-ethical similarities.

Take the classic example of killing a child. Even the merciless killing of children to avenge some wrong is done because the one seeking vengeance chooses to hurt his or her enemy in the worst way by taking that which is most precious to him. In other words, the child was killed, not because its life was worthless, but because the child's life was esteemed to be of greatest value. (The very establishment of law and order in any community is because of the realization that without law and order plunder and savagery prevail.)

The problem with dismissing all guilt as cultural is that morality becomes untenable. No one can honestly be willing to concede to that position for to do so would be self-defeating.

A Universal Story

Many years ago when I was in Cambodia I personally witnessed what historians are calling "the murder of a gentle land." Over several years the people there have suffered much at the hands of murderous demagogues. That small nation has lost millions to the cause of one political theory or another.

One evening, some missionaries and my interpreter asked me if I would like to see a play. Eager for a break from the meetings I was addressing, I took them up on the offer. Attending a theatrical performance in a land struggling for survival was a very moving experience. There was a strange combination of escape and reality in the meager surroundings of the ill-cared-for theater. The story in the play was equally a cross between fact and fancy. It was the story of a young peasant who married a lovely young village woman. As they were blissfully on their journey to another village to set up their own home the prince of the land, traveling with his soldiers, was captured by her beauty and demanded that the peasant give her to him as a palace concubine. The peasant resisted valiantly, and so by force, the prince grabbed the woman and took her away with him.

Dismayed and heartsick, the peasant hastened to the palace to beg the king to intercede for him and to return his wife. The king was outraged by the poor man's charge and contended that the woman came by her own volition to live with the prince. To prove his point, the king ordered the woman to be brought to a palace hearing. When she was led before him he demanded that she acknowledge who her real husband was. The moment of truth came, and all were gathered in the palace hall to hear her words.

Behind the scene, of course, the king had threatened the woman that if she admitted that the peasant was indeed her husband he would be taken away and killed. The woman therefore, in great fear, when challenged by the authority in the court softly but with evident trepidation pointed to the prince as her actual husband. The court went into an uproar, cheering the king as the peasant cowered under the weight of this rejection.

The priest watching these proceedings demanded an inquiry and then announced to the people that something seemed wrong with the whole scenario. "Why would an ordinary man risk the rage of the king by claiming that the prince's wife was his? I have the perfect solution to get to the truth," he said.

He then proceeded to lay out a simple plan based on what he claimed was a foolproof truth serum. "I will give both the prince and the peasant an equal dose of this serum and within ten minutes the effect will take place. Knowing that one of them is telling a lie and will be punished by death for that crime, I suggest that each of these men be given five minutes alone with the woman, with no physical contact between them."

A huge barrel suspended from the midpoint of a pole held horizontally was brought to the stage. It was so large it took two people, one shouldering each end of the pole, to carry this unwieldy equipment. The instructions were then given. The woman was to carry one end of the pole while each of the men in turn was to carry the other end, separated by the barrel. They could walk away to a secluded setting prior to returning for the verdict. Each had five minutes with the woman.

During the time she had with the prince he did nothing but harangue her and threaten her with her husband's death if she ever spoke the truth. When the time came for her to be alone with her husband, it was fascinating to watch even the subtle hints of his love for her. He did his best to position himself so that he would carry the brunt of the weight of the barrel and protect her from any strain. During the time they were alone she wept and spoke of her undying love for him and explained that the only reason she had lied was to spare his life.

"If they had threatened my life I could take it, but I could not bear to see you die," she said. He understood her plight and said that he would only speak the truth.

They returned to a suspense-filled courtroom, and I might add, to an audience filled even more with anticipation, all of us sitting at the edge of our seats. As all was readied for the serum to take effect, the priest announced that the truth would now triumph over the lie. At that moment the barrel burst open and out jumped a little boy who had been hiding inside. He carried a pen and pad in his hand and had copied down all he had heard during the private conversations the men had when each was alone with the woman.

The young boy turned over his notes to the priest. The priest read what they contained, and as he watched the prince lower his head and the peasant's face shine with the radiance of a returned love, he declared the truth. The audience in the auditorium could not contain its jubilation and roared with approval, only to see tragedy strike as the king ordered his soldiers to kill all who believed the young boy's version of the conversations.

Anyone in Cambodia knew the double-edged tragedy of the play. The voice of truth had been silenced, and cruel men ruled the land, inflicting fear on the people. I sat silently even after the play was over and reflected how behind the drama lay some common values that bind humanity: The purity of marital love. The value of the truth. The cry to protect the innocent. The wickedness of unbridled power and the undying yearning of a people to see justice roll on like a river. These were not conferred culturally. These truths were self-evident even in a Marxist-dominated land.

I was quite taken by the story and overwhelmed with the almost childlike innocence with which the people discussed the story together as they left the theater. Families pondered the deeper truths. Couples exchanged views on what they had liked and disliked about the play. Clearly there was a trumpet sound for honor and morality behind the whole tale. Thus, to do away with guilt as purely a cultural distinctive, valued by some and not by others, does not reflect the reality of our shared experience.

We have looked at four options for responding to guilt: To expel all guilt by irreverence makes life unlivable. To smother it by pride makes one's attitude unaccountable. To conceal guilt by fear makes life unbearable. To dismiss guilt as cultural makes morality untenable.

DENY GUILT BY INNOCENCE

This brings us to the fifth and possibly the most insidious option, and that is to not feel *any* guilt because one has lived a life as best as is possible. If a life is so well lived, what is the reason for personal guilt? There are multitudes who so live under the illusion of innocence. Repentance is not a necessary concept within their framework.

In some cultures where their heroes are revered as if they were almost gods, I have been asked countless times a question that is intended to make the Christian faith look unfair: "Are you saying that so and so, who lived such a good life, will be in hell?"

The unstated question often behind such a conundrum is often never really admitted. What the questioner in some cases tries to imply is that there is no such thing as hell. I am often tempted to ask whether the questioner himself has led a life as good as the one whose name he has raised as symbolizing saintliness. If hell is exempted for "good" people, what happens to the "bad" ones? Are they content with even that reality, that the "bad" indeed have a godless destiny? How many "good" ones are there?

Malcolm Muggeridge once said that the depravity of man is the most empirically verifiable fact but also the most resisted by the human mind. If the complaint is made that in Christianity heaven is restricted to those who trust in Christ and is therefore limited, I shudder to think of how few there will be in heaven if goodness determined that number. I ask again, therefore, Is there a veiled denial of all judgment behind the query? Even where that may not be the intent, in Christian terms the answer is quite straightforward. Jesus did not come into this world to make bad people good. He came into this world to make dead people live. Those who were dead to God were to be made alive to Him through the work of the Holy Spirit.

But the point goes beyond that. Once again we might ask, what are we talking about when we mean *good?* Is it up to each person's own definition? And if it is, why do we deny everyone else the right to have his or her own definition of good? There is only one who has the right to define good, and that is God. The Scriptures tell us that our condition is measured not by how we fare against each other but that we fall short of the standard of God (see Rom. 3:23). Millions of microbes exist in our world outside of our sight. Bring a microscope to bear upon an object, and a world unseen suddenly startles the mind as it comes into view. Under God's eyes what duplicities are uncovered and what sickness of the soul is visible that we never saw on our own?

That is precisely why the gospel message is not a message whereby we earn our salvation or our way into heaven. Such a concept is completely out of keeping with what God offers to us. We make a cardinal mistake when we weigh our merit before God in terms of volume rather than in terms of our condition before Him. Our "lostness" is the greatest when we think we do not need God's grace, not because we were part of some great scheme of exterminating humanity. Jesus reserved His sternest reminder to the one who claimed goodness before God, not to the one who wept as a sinner.

Fyodor Dostoevsky told the story of a woman who died and went to hell. Rather perturbed by that end state of hers, she challenged the heavens to give her a reason why she was not there. Hearing her screams of injustice, Peter spoke to her and said, "Tell me one reason why you should be in heaven."

She paused, rehearsed, thought through carefully, and then said, "On one occasion I gave a beggar a carrot."

Peter checked the ledger and saw that she had indeed done so. It was a scrawny old spoiled carrot, but she had nevertheless given it. Peter told her to hold on, that they would help her up. He took a long string, tied a carrot to the end of it, and lowered it into hell for her to hold on to. She clung to it, and he started to pull her up. Others in hell saw her gradually disappearing from their midst and held on to her ankles so that they could be transported, too. As more and more of them kept clinging on, the string started to give way, and she yelled out with every fiber of her being, "Leave go of me! This is my carrot, not yours." As soon as she said that, the carrot broke.

Even the best of deeds can be self-serving, and we all need that grace of God to enter His presence. The most virtuous in this world are not too virtuous to need God's grace, and no one is so virtuous as to reserve the right to be the sole definer of goodness. That is God's prerogative. Claiming complete innocence in the eyes of God is unjustifiable.

This leaves only one way to deal legitimately and reasonably with the problem of guilt.

SURRENDER GUILT TO GOD'S GRACE

Just as the fact of Eichmann's hatred drove home the condition of the human heart with greater significance than did the fiction of George Steiner, without mitigating the reality behind each story, so also the real-life incident of King David put alongside the fiction of the Cambodian play brings the truth home with double force. I am referring to the story of David when he was confronted by Nathan regarding his adulterous relationship with Bathsheba.

After Nathan had presented the parable of the man with many sheep who had stolen the one lamb of another, David could not resist pronouncing judgment on that heartless thief. "That man should surely die," said David. He spoke too soon, going on the basis of the unjustifiable act. Nathan's stare must have been devastating to David when it was followed by the words, "Thou art the man" (2 Sam. 12:7 KJV).

Think of the number of ways David could have dealt with his guilt. He could have had Nathan arrested and killed. He could have blamed Bathsheba. He could have claimed the divine right of kings. He could have abrogated the seventh commandment. Kings across history have made such choices. Irreverence, pride, and other machinations could have played a part here. Instead, he fell on his face before God and cried out:

> Have mercy upon me, O God,
>   according to your unfailing love;
> according to your great compassion
>   blot out my transgressions.
> Wash away all my iniquity
>   and cleanse me from my sin.
>
> For I know my transgressions,
>   and my sin is always before me.
> Against you, you only have I sinned
>   and done what is evil in your sight,
> so that you are proved right when you speak
>   and justified when you judge. . . .
> Surely you desire truth in the inner parts; . . .
> Cleanse me . . . ;
>   wash me . . . .
> Let me hear joy and gladness;
>   let the bones you have crushed rejoice. . . .
>
> You do not delight in sacrifice, or I would bring it; . . .
>   The sacrifices of God are a broken spirit;
>   a broken and contrite heart,
>   O God, you will not despise. (Ps. 51:1–8, 16–17)

There is not a more familiar psalm of contrition. Here the worst of wrongdoing and guilt found forgiveness and peace. We need to be sure of one thing. This is not a cheap prayer of self-justification. David was going to pay dearly for his sin in the wounds that he had inflicted upon his nation and upon himself. He would lose that child that he so desperately wished could live. But David's heart was mended by understanding the grievousness of sin and by the cleansing touch of God.

Let us return to the tragic saga of Jim Bakker and the tragedy of PTL. I know of no better and more potent illustration in our time. Few will forget the sadness and, for some, the outrage they experienced when the story broke and the empire fell. Shortly after the sordid facts of immorality and coverup by some in the PTL leadership were exposed, the press reporter who had played a key role in disclosing the story titled his book with irony and sarcasm *Forgiven.* The revulsion felt by many was not hidden. How could one claim forgiveness by just uttering a few words, most of which were self-justifying? None except the guilty could have considered that fair.

But some time ago I found myself standing a few feet away from Mr. Bakker. Recently released from serving a humiliating prison term, he looked only a shadow of his former self as he stood alone, for the most part, and only a few stopped to greet him. It was hard not to feel some of his pain even as I looked in his direction. That evening he spoke to an audience at the Christian Booksellers Association. He spoke of his heartache and of his duplicity as a result of which he lost everything—his wife, his ministry, his reputation. He spoke of a dismal day in prison when everything seemed dark. He was cleaning the toilets when he was told that a guest had come to see him. Looking at himself in that unpleasant clothing and condition, he wondered if he really could go and meet anyone. But recognizing his true state—that this is what he had descended to—he went to the meeting room completely unaware of who his guest would be. Little did he realize what awaited him. He was ushered into the room and stopped in a state of shock to see Billy Graham reach out to him and embrace him.

How rich is this illustration of grace; a man who over a lifetime has won the admiration of millions for being above the seduction of money and sensuality reaching out to embrace a man upon whom the masses had vented such anger for having failed the public trust in those very areas. But those who stop there miss the larger point. The grace of Billy Graham's forgiveness was only an outflow of the grace he himself has enjoyed and that each one of us enjoys when we come to Christ for forgiveness. It was the same grace offered to Jim Bakker even as it preceded the appropriately titled book *I Was Wrong.* That should have been written first, and then *Forgiven* could have been written, not in irony, but in song. It is the song of the soul set free.

Sin scorches us most after we receive the grace of forgiveness, not before. The forgiven one realizes the gravity of the sin more when he or she is genuinely repentant and has been forgiven. God beckons our crying hearts to come to Him in repentance. This makes our sin forgivable.

When expelled by irreverence, guilt makes life in mutual harmony unlivable. When smothered by pride it makes one's life unaccountable. When concealed by fear it makes the pain unbearable. When dismissed as cultural it makes morality untenable. When claiming absolute innocence before God it makes the claim unjustifiable. *When guilt surrenders to the grace of God, it makes the sin forgivable.* John Newton knew what he was talking about when he wrote, "Amazing grace, how sweet the sound/That saved a wretch like me!"

Simon Wiesenthal's predicament was a genuine one, but so was the hell of the Nazi soldier who was desperate for forgiveness. One can fully sympathize with Mr. Wiesenthal's reticence to deal with so great a crime in so simple a manner. But there is nothing simple about God's forgiveness. With all its grandeur and splendor, the temple had a bloody side to it—the sacrifice of bulls and goats in an effort to find cleansing and forgiveness.

I recall standing by the altar of the Temple of Kali in Calcutta, India. I saw a man dressed in spotless white clothing bring a small goat tied by a rope. At the altar, the head of the goat was placed upon a contraption that cradled its head. Then, faster than the eye could see, the priest's knife had done its work, and the animal was sacrificed. But then something strange happened. The man placed his own head on the same spot, bent down, touched some of the freshly spilled blood, and marked a spot upon his white shirt before he left.

I turned to a Hindu philosopher who happened to be showing us around and asked him what that symbolic gesture meant. Quite embarrassed, he shook off the question saying, "It does not mean anything." Rather a bizarre act, I might add, for something that means absolutely nothing.

Such has been the quest of religion. The Hindu pays his Karma through millions of reincarnations. The Muslim intones hopefully, "Insh Allah"—if God wills—and even at death never knows any certainty of forgiveness. But the one who comes to the cross of Christ knows with certainty that the debt has been paid. This is the grace of God that faces the guilty one head-on and is big enough to forgive. The guilt is eradicated completely.

THE SAVIOR'S SOLUTION

You may or may not have noticed that on our way to a solution for how to respond to guilt a very subtle though enormous chasm was crossed before forgiveness was offered. The focus shifted away from guilt.

Ingmar Bergman may have captured this huge chasm better than even he realized in his play *Wild Strawberries.* It is the story of a professor who had come before a judge to be sentenced. The judge looked at the accused and declared, "I find you guilty."

"Guilty of what?" demanded the professor.

"You are guilty of guilt," said the judge.

"Is that serious?" asked the accused man.

"Very serious," answered the judge.

Think for a moment. If guilt is all we have to deal with, where do we go? How does one remove guilt?

"Not all the perfumes of Arabia," said Lady Macbeth, "can remove this spot."

"This disease is beyond my cure," says the doctor.

Reincarnations and uncertainty plague the religiously minded. Who are we going to beckon to our bedsides? Can guilt just be erased with a word? If only one can take the next step and say, "I am guilty of *sin*," then the answer comes triumphantly—"Ah! I have a Savior for you." He went to the cross to carry that penalty and pay our price. It was not cheap; it was God's priceless gift of His Son to bear the guilt brought by the sin of the world.

I have a friend who years ago spoke to me of how difficult a lesson it was for him when he learned the cost of forgiveness. He had betrayed his wife and family and lived through the pain of asking for forgiveness and rebuilding their trust. Somehow over a period of time he assumed that even for them, the hurt was all mended and the past expunged from their memory. One day he returned home from work early in the afternoon, just to get a break. He walked into the house, and when he entered could hear his wife, who was on her knees crying, unaware that he was home, asking God to help her forget all that had brought her this pain.

It was a rude awakening to him of the cost. Multiply that wrong by a limitless number, and you will get a glimpse of what Christ bore on the cross for you and for me.

When the play in Cambodia was over, I asked my interpreter, "So much went wrong. What was missing in this story?"

Though he was not a Christian he gave me an answer I was not expecting. He said without hesitation, "A Savior."

Guilt is a real experience of life. But when it remains as just guilt it is compounded by each self-serving effort of irreverence, pride, fear, dismissal of the moral, or the claim of innocence. Only in the admission of sin is there a genuine restoration, because guilt is first a vertical problem before it is a horizontal one. God is the one who has been violated before humanity has been wronged. That is why only God has the ultimate prerogative to forgive. Only then is guilt eradicated completely. Only then can the one who has been forgiven know what it is to receive and in turn offer forgiveness when wronged. We are all weary of living in a world that lives with the logic of unforgiveness.

How grand in its place is the forgiveness of God that we may receive personally.

The well-known lines of John Donne express so beautifully the comprehensiveness and the thrill of such grace provided by Jesus Christ when one acknowledges that he or she is guilty of sin.

> Wilt Thou forgive that sin where I begun,
>   Which was my sin, though it were done before?
> Wilt Thou forgive that sin through which I run,
>   And do run still, though still I do deplore?
> When Thou hast done, Thou hast not done;
>   For I have more.
>
> Wilt Thou forgive that sin which I have won
>   Others to sin, and made my sins their door?
> Wilt Thou forgive that sin which I did shun
>   A year or two, but wallowed in a score?
> When Thou hast done, Thou hast not done;
>   For I have more.
>
> I have a sin of fear, that when I've spun
>   My last thread, I shall perish on the shore;
> But swear by Thyself that at my death Thy Son
>   Shall shine as He shines now and heretofore:
> And having done that, Thou hast not done;
>   I fear no more.[11]

Five

The Cry for Freedom in Pleasure

TO SOME OF MY READERS this story will be familiar. But it helps me frame more clearly the nature of the subject before us and its importance. Years ago, our family was traveling home from Toronto, Canada. Our daughter Sarah had just undergone some very critical and intricate surgery in her inner ear. Her head was all bandaged up as a result, and she was recovering very well.

We stopped en route at a relative's place and spent the afternoon on a mini-golf course for the children to have a time of fun together. Suddenly our son came running to us, shouting, "Mom! Mom! Hurry and come! Sarah is hurt!"

We were sure that she had somehow reinjured that ear. But when we ran up to her we were to see a rather pitiful sight that as a family we will never forget. She was kneeling on the ground with her face in her hands while blood poured through her fingers. She was crying out in pain as she repeated, "Help me!"

An accidental full-blooded swing of a golf club had caught her directly on the eye and left that side of the face dreadfully hurt. We rushed her to the hospital in an ambulance, nursing many questions as we faced the grim possibility of a lost eye. In His abundant grace God spared her that. The emergency surgery was an extraordinary success and has left her unscarred such that no one would ever know how critical it was at one stage. Life changes with such close calls.

Experiences like that which wound or hurt are multiplied millions of times in the human situation. That is why we are prompted time and again to raise the question of pain and suffering. But I have wondered long and hard why it is that while we relentlessly seek God's answers when in the throes of suffering we never seem to pause with equal sincerity to ask Him for guidance or wisdom in pleasure and seem very uncertain about God's presence in fun and pleasure.

Is it not also instructive of our bias that society popularly brands all tragedies as "acts of God" but fails to attribute equal credit when we enjoy something good? This is a reversal of Job's predicament. He knew that all good came from God but was puzzled at the source of all bad. We postmodern skeptics blame God for all the bad and credit ourselves with all that is good. Have we all bought into a belief that God is not interested in making life enjoyable? Has the Christian faith somehow been molded and reshaped to appear as a killer of pleasure or as a barrier to fun? Have enjoyment and amusement now been handed over to "the world" so that the very idea of pleasure is seen as inimical to spirituality? Can God give to us a wide array of pleasures including the physical and the aesthetic that we may enjoy without feeling that it is a break from the routine for the Christian?

There are very few issues in as much need of being thought through and carefully addressed as this one. Nobody denies that the variety of pleasures that is offered up to our consumer culture has opened up once unthinkable possibilities in staggering proportions. Billions of dollars are spent in the pleasure industry, appealing to anything from the delightful to the offensive, the cerebral to the sensual, the informative to the unconscionable. Sights, sounds, images, tastes, things, passions, and experiences abound, all offered up in glittering and alluring array. We have in our hands some of the finest technology, and what creative genius could do with all of this is something worth pondering. For after all, we do have a need to be entertained and have fun. That explains the success from the beginning of human experience of anything that captures and provokes the imagination.

A MIXED BLESSING

Since this need for pleasure is undeniably true, questions galore emerge. How do we find genuine freedom to enjoy life in its best offerings? How do we choose that which is legitimate pleasure and reject that which is illegitimate? More to the point, how do we learn to think on these matters constructively rather than to live pragmatically, making momentary decisions without guiding principles that will inform our choices?

Of particular concern to millions is the frustration that is felt in knowing how to guide our children and young people, for theirs is a world of limitless opportunities. What deep struggles and questions must engulf them as they are fed a steady diet of all that appeals to the eye and the imagination, with so little to nurture the conscience. They are being manipulated into the belief that appetite is sufficient reason to consume anything. And what is worse, new appetites are being created that leave them hungrier than before and under the illusion that those hungers could be met if one could only remove all restraint.

One shudders to think of the damage done to them long before they have the maturity and inner strength to glean the good and to reject the lies. The ramifications of the capacity locked into cyberspace has brought new possibilities even for children. What image, what idea, what language, what invasion will take place in minds so tender? All pleasure does not come with a warning label. Neither the Supreme Court nor law can change the wills that are determined to market their products that offer pleasure without restraint and destroy people without apology.

But let us pause before we get carried away. I think here we do ourselves a tremendous injustice when we find the entertainment media to be the easy target. They deserve a portion of the blame, yes, but not all of it. Such bashing can be the emotional way out of something that is far too complex a web, which we have all shared in spinning. Besides, pleasure is not just exclusively in their domain. The sources are numerous, and the possibilities are a blend of the beautiful and the contemptible.

A FORMIDABLE CHALLENGE

What role, for example, have intellectuals played in this dance with an unfettered lifestyle? Have they been any less a force in causing young minds to stumble? The reality is that there is nothing so vulgar left in human experience that some educator from somewhere cannot be flown in to justify. In the name of literary license and propelled by a celebrated relativism, anything passes off as normal—just call it diversity in our culture, and that is reason enough.

Nearly thirty years ago, Malcolm Muggeridge's resignation from his chaplaincy at the University of Edinburgh was fueled by a moral struggle, principally the request of students that the university play a role in supplying them with contraceptives. Here is what Muggeridge said in his farewell address:

> So, dear Edinburgh students, this may well be the last time I address you, and this is what I want to say—and I don't really care whether it means anything to you or not, whether you think there is anything in it or not. I want you to believe that this row I have had with your elected officers has nothing to do with any puritanical attitudes on my part. I have no belief in abstinence for abstinence's own sake, no wish under any circumstances to check any fulfillment of your life and being. But I have to say to you this: that whatever life is or is not about, it is not to be expressed in terms of drug stupefaction and casual sexual relations. However we may venture into the unknown it is not I assure you on the plastic wings of *Playboy* magazine or psychedelic fancies.[1]

Little did he dream then what modern-day learning was going to do even to those younger than in universities. But thankfully the world of education is not completely silent on this downward slide. From within its ranks there are voices calling us to caution and to think through carefully what lies before us. That is worthy of applause and appreciation.

In 1985, Neil Postman, one of those voices, had this to say in the preface of his book *Amusing Ourselves to Death,* as he contrasted George Orwell's *1984* and Aldous Huxley's *Brave New World:*

> What Orwell feared were those who would ban books. What Huxley feared was that there would be no reason to ban a book, for there would be no one who would want to read one. Orwell feared those who would deprive us of information. Huxley feared those who would give us so much that we would be reduced to passivity and egoism. Orwell feared that the truth would be concealed from us. Huxley feared the truth would be drowned in a sea of irrelevance. Orwell feared we would become a captive culture. Huxley feared that we would become a trivial culture, preoccupied with some equivalent of the feelies, the orgy porgy, and the centrifugal bumblepuppy. As Huxley remarked in *Brave New World Revisited,* the civil libertarians and rationalists who are ever on the alert to oppose tyranny "failed to take into account man's almost infinite appetite for distractions." In *1984,* Huxley added, people are controlled by inflicting pain. In *Brave New World,* they are controlled by inflicting pleasure. In short, Orwell feared that what we hate will ruin us. Huxley feared that what we love will ruin us. This book is about the possibility that Huxley, not Orwell, was right.[2]

AN UNCERTAIN SOUND

Postman is right. But here again, we must stop and take stock. The media are easy targets. The impact of secular education is far more daunting, but that too can be made a whipping post on any moralizing platform. Given their starting points, it is not surprising that both those institutions will flirt with such dangers. There is, in truth, a more painful recognition than to direct criticism against either the media or secular education. The church as a whole must bear some of the blame, because we have been so delinquent by not addressing this problem in depth. Particular pleasures, yes. They have been hammered again and again by all of us. But there is an evident dearth of instruction providing underlying principles that can guide us through some tough terrain. If one were to add to this absence the disconcerting truth that survey after survey is showing that in our private lives there is very little difference between those who claim to be followers of Christ and those who don't, then the reason for our troubled scene becomes alarmingly clear.

It was a disillusioned Freud, of all people, who said early in the century, "I have found little that is good about human beings on the whole. In my experience most of them are trash no matter whether they publicly subscribe to this or that ethical doctrine or to none at all."[3] Somewhat harsh and overstated maybe, but not completely off the mark. We all, if we are honest, flounder for lack of clear direction and inner strength in a world of changing and multiplying options.

But if pleasure is meant to be legitimate and God Himself speaks to us of the wisdom that we need to rescue ourselves from legalism in one extreme and to free ourselves to enjoy life in the best sense of the term, the question emerges: How can we find the delights that our hearts yearn for without victimizing ourselves in the process? How can life be enjoyed without profaning it in the process?

Once we glean what God invites us to, we find that the imagination harnessed by God can be a wellspring of enthrallment. There is the pleasure of listening. The pleasure of seeing. The pleasure of taste and touch. The pleasure of feeling and knowing and ultimately, of course, the pleasure of being.

Take the simple yet grand experience of human sexuality in its consummate expression between man and wife. Mindless evolution could never have brought such delight to the human soul and body. In His omnipotence God could have rendered it nothing more than a procreative act. That wonder of a new life would have been miraculous enough. But instead He has blessed the consummation with the supreme pleasure of love, of tenderness, and of enjoyment. Would this God who made such ecstasy in purity possible, deny us direction in pleasure? Thankfully not. Let us plumb the depths as best as we can. I believe the answers we will find as we now pursue this question will be both thrilling and practical.

FRAMING THE PROBLEM

One author who did address this theme, well before our time, was the great English essayist F. W. Boreham. Writing a half-century ago, his insights were outstanding. He accurately portrays the torment of being caught between the legalistic castigations of those determined to make all pleasure a curse of the flesh and the lawless indulgences of those pursuing pleasure and fun as ends in themselves. This is how he worded our predicament:

> Laughter, merriment and fun were quite evidently intended to occupy a large place in this world. Yet on no subject under the sun has the church displayed more embarrassment and confusion. One might almost suppose that here we have discovered an important phase of human experience on which Christianity is criminally reticent; a "terra incognita" which no intrepid prophet had explored; a silent sea upon whose waters no ecclesiastical adventurer had ever burst; a dark and eerie country upon which no sun had ever shone. Dr. Jowett tells us of the devout old Scotsman who, on Saturday night, locked up the piano and unlocked the organ, reversing the process last thing on the Sabbath evening. The piano is the sinner; the organ the saint! Dr. Parker used to wax merry at the man who regarded bagatelle as a gift from heaven, whilst billiards he deemed to be a stepping stone to perdition. The play we condemn; it is anathema to us. The same play—or a vastly inferior one screened on a film, we delightedly admire. One Christian follows the round

> of gaiety with the maddest of the merry; another wears a hair shirt, and starves himself into a skeleton. One treats life as all a frolic; another as all a funeral. We swerve from the Scylla of aestheticism to the Charybdis of asceticism. We swing like a pendulum from the indulgence of the Epicurean to the severities of the Stoic, failing to recognize, with the author of *Ecce Homo,* that it is the glory of Christianity that, rejecting the absurdities of each, it combines the cardinal excellencies of both. We allow without knowing why we allow; we ban without knowing why we prohibit. We
>
> Compound for sins we are inclined to
> By damning those we have no mind to.
>
> We are at sea without chart or compass. Our theories of pleasure are in hopeless confusion. Is there no definite doctrine of amusement? Is there no philosophy of fun? There must be! And there is![4]

Is there no doctrine of amusement? Is there no philosophy of fun? Boreham asks. Does it not sound like a collection of oxymorons? Doctrine and amusement. Philosophy and fun. Thankfully there is a doctrine of pleasure because pleasure is not only a result—it also has its boundaries. This is not to bring limits as much as to protect us from enslavement. There is a philosophy of fun, because fun is not only a physical activity but is based on that which has been thought through. And contrary to most prejudice, thinking can be fun, too. The Bible addresses pleasure possibly far more than it does the issue of pain, because the truth is that ultimately meaninglessness does not come from being weary of pain, but meaninglessness comes from being weary of pleasure. Solomon wrestled with the issue possibly more than anyone else. He was a specialist in pleasure. But he came to some firm and confident conclusions:

> I thought in my heart, "Come now, I will test you with pleasure to find out what is good." But that also proved to be meaningless.

> "Laughter," I said, "is foolish. And what does pleasure accomplish?" I tried cheering myself with wine and embracing folly—my mind still guiding me with wisdom. I wanted to see what was worthwhile for men to do under heaven during the few days of their lives.
>
> I undertook great projects: I built homes for myself and planted vineyards. I made gardens and parks and planted all kinds of fruit trees in them. I made reservoirs to water groves of flourishing trees. I bought male and female slaves and had other slaves who were born in my house. I also owned more herds and flocks than anyone in Jerusalem before me. I amassed silver and gold for myself, and the treasure of kings and provinces. I acquired men and women singers, and a harem as well—the delights of the heart of man. I became greater by far than anyone in Jerusalem before me. In all this my wisdom stayed with me.
>
> I denied myself nothing my eyes desired;
> I refused my heart no pleasure.
> My heart took delight in all my work,
> and this was the reward for all my labor.
> Yet when I surveyed all that my hands had done
> and what I had toiled to achieve,
> everything was meaningless, a chasing after the wind;
> nothing was gained under the sun. (Eccles. 2:1–11)

When novelist Jack Higgins was asked what he now knows that he wishes he had known when he was young, he said, "I wish somebody had told me then that when you get to the top there's nothing there." Solomon, in far more radical terms, proved that a long time ago.

Here we see our first warning sign. Does this not come as a surprise that after years of experimenting and indulging in everything the eye could procure Solomon came to the conclusion that his life of unlimited pleasure left him empty and cynical? Was he not the dean of pleasure seekers? He took hedonism to new extremes.

The seventh chapter of the Book of Proverbs is a dramatic reminder of his own entrapment. But let us take very careful note. Solomon's was not just a harem-filled world of sensuality; he was a genius in artistic strength. He wrote profusely and aspired to great heights in literature, in architecture, in music, and in philosophy. Thousands of proverbs and songs flowed from his pen. We miscast him if we forget that he had an immense creative capacity. Centuries later we still see the remains of his accomplishments. But in these words, Solomon foreshadowed all who would follow in his train. His experience has been replicated in thousands of lives. Like a purveyor of pornography who becomes impotent or a gambler who picks his own pockets, unrestrained pleasure has plundered its own lovers.

Sustaining this very thought, psychologists Frank Minirth and Paul Meier in their book *Happiness Is a Choice* say this:

> Dr. Minirth and I are convinced that many people do choose happiness but still do *not* obtain it. The reason for this is that even though they choose to be happy, they seek for inner peace and joy in the wrong places. They seek for happiness in materialism and do not find it. They seek for joy in sexual prowess but end up with fleeting pleasures and bitter long-term disappointments. They seek inner fulfillment by obtaining positions of power in corporations, in government, or even in their own families (by exercising excessive control), but they remain unfulfilled. I have had millionaire businessmen come to my office and tell me they have big houses, yachts, condominiums in Colorado, nice children, a beautiful mistress, an unsuspecting wife, secure corporate positions—and suicidal tendencies. They have everything this world has to offer except one thing—inner peace and joy. They come to my office as a last resort, begging me to help them conquer the urge to kill themselves. Why? The answers are not simple. The human mind and emotions are a very complex, dynamic system.[5]

Such irony is a very difficult reality to absorb and to believe for the average person. This alone ought to cause us to stop and take note that where unbridled pleasure abounds there is greater need to find answers, lest our own lives spend themselves into emptiness.

THE WISDOM WE SEEK

But there is one enormous clue that Solomon gives to us as he leads us in the right direction. "Under the sun," he said, everything was "a chasing after the wind." Under the sun means an existence outside of God where there is no input from outside—a closed system. What else can the secular media do but dabble in weirder concoctions of the senses when their philosophy is bred under the sun? What else can secular education do when its intellect is sold out to a closed system?

But for the Christian, God has spoken. Our theory of pleasure is not born from under the sun but from Him who the psalmist says has "set [His] glory above the heavens" (Ps. 8:1) and who sent us His Son, whose life has been the benchmark of all that is good. Yet He spoke of a joy that rises above anything this world under the sun has to offer.

As he sought to answer his own questions, "Is there no definite doctrine of amusement? Is there no philosophy of fun?" F. W. Boreham gave us three fundamental principles that he felt would provide the wisdom we needed in the midst of our choices. Naturally, he draws them from the Scriptures. I shall underscore them, expand upon them, and then add to them.

Legitimate Pleasure

The first principle Boreham gleans from a very remote passage. It does not address the issue directly but clearly has the principle couched inside. The backdrop is the story of Gideon preparing to fight against the Midianites. In Judges 7 we are told of the looming battle. The Israelites had gathered an army of formidable size, wanting to make certain of victory, when God interrupted their march with a confounding statement. He told Gideon that his thirty-two-thousand-man army was just too big and that he was to reduce the number drastically. When

Gideon gave permission for those men who were afraid to leave, twenty-two thousand accepted his offer and left.

But God said, "You still have too many."

Now came the unsuspecting moment after which Gideon was left with just three hundred soldiers. He paused in the march to allow them to take a drink from a nearby river, and the manner in which they drank, to which they were oblivious, became the standard for selection. We shall not go into that methodological difference of ingesting water; rather, we will salvage a very subtle but definite truth that emerges.

This is the principle. There was nothing wrong with a pause to take a drink of water. It refreshed them without taking them away from the reason they were there or from where they were headed in the first place. **Any pleasure that refreshes you without diminishing you, distracting you, or sidetracking you from the ultimate goal is a legitimate pleasure.**

What this clearly means is that there is a fundamental prerequisite for defining any legitimate pleasure in life, any freedom that we enjoy, and that is to first establish the purpose of life itself. All pleasure is built upon why you and I exist in the first place. If only we could grasp this truth, how many hours and years of grief would be spared us. God never intended for life to be lived out on an *ad hoc* basis, taking each opportunity as an isolated choice. Life is not to be regarded as a smorgasbord of appetizers placed before us from which we can unconscionably choose or reject with equal impunity; it must be defined first, and on the basis of that definition we are to make the right choices that will truly delight and not destroy. The undergirding philosophy of life has to be the point of reference for all choices. That is what helps us distinguish between fulfillment and disappointment, between fun and destructiveness.

Every corporation first defines its purpose then establishes the structure and the means by which that mission is to be maximized. Life's purpose must also be first set in place before the best way to live it out is determined.

This was the rationale behind Danish philosopher Sören Kierkegaard's statement that he had learned to define life backward and live it forward. By that he meant that the destiny he sought became the dictator of the direction to choose. He started from the final state of life from which to determine the present path chosen. That is the legitimate way to begin any journey.

Growing up in India, I recall taking part in a strange event called the slow cycling race during a community sports day. The goal of the race was not to take off as soon as the gun sounded but to move as slowly as you could. In fact, it was even better if you could remain standing still on your bicycle with your feet not touching the ground. In other words, the goal of the race was to come in last. Some were so adept at staying stationary that the distance of the race was only a few yards.

I can just imagine some visitor who happened to be a cycling champion in his own country walking by and taking a look at the cyclists positioning themselves for the start, and thinking, "I wish I could be in that race and teach these novices a thing or two about cycling." If out of courtesy he were offered that opportunity, just imagine his utter astonishment when at the sound of the gun he sped off and breasted the tape seconds later only to turn around and see the rest still at the starting line in a test of balancing a motionless bike. And then imagine his shock to discover that he was *last* for having reached the finish line *first.* It pays to know the purpose of a race or of life so that you can play by the rules and win.

Susannah Wesley had precisely this purpose in mind when she answered her son John's request for a definition of sin. Bear in mind that she had nineteen children; therefore her words were well chosen, knowing she was raising a veritable community in her home. She said:

> Whatever weakens your reasoning, impairs the tenderness of your conscience, obscures your sense of God or takes away your relish for spiritual things; in short, if anything increases the authority and the power of the flesh over the spirit, that to you becomes sin, however good it is in itself.[6]

If the primary goal of life is a closer walk with God, then even the good is sometimes set aside in favor of the best.

Losing Sight of the Goal

Few characters in the Bible evoke as much consternation as Samson. His recurring failure lay in his inability to align his life with the purpose for which God had formed him. We read in Judges 13 that his parents had been sent an angelic messenger to inform them of the unique role God had determined for Samson. Bringing up children is a demanding and life-consuming task. How much greater is the pressure of shaping a life that you know will in turn shape the history of a nation. With that solemn charge before them, they taught him the inestimable value of responsible choices.

Yet Samson could never tame his passions and bring them under the control of his greater call. He faltered when he fell in love with a Philistine woman and insisted that his parents "get her for me." The tone and the erratic demand of Samson spoke volumes. His father pled with him to bear in mind that God had raised him up with the specific charge to defend his people against the Philistine threat. How could he possibly not run into conflict if he married from among the very people who were his sworn enemies and from whom he was to protect his nation? Samson shunned that warning and crossed the line.

He stumbled awhile later when he was lured into the bed of a prostitute. He fell and wrecked himself when Delilah toyed with him until he betrayed his sacred trust before God. The Scriptures tell us of the moment of reckoning that came. Having compromised all his convictions one after another, he audaciously believed that he still had the strength God had given to him. Instead, his enemies humiliated him. How ironic was that final moment when he needed the eyes of a young lad to lead him to the pillars of the Philistine temple. All this because he had lost sight of God's purpose for his life.

If a person does not understand that the purpose of life defines lifestyle, then the lifestyle itself is hollow and the life is squandered.

Samson ought not to have been in the places he frequented, and he ought not to have flirted with the people that he did.

This simple fact has deep ramifications. The places to which we go, the friendships we embrace, the language we use, the shows we watch, the books we read, the thoughts we entertain—all must be aligned with the purpose to which we are called by God. A bank manager who comes upon an unauthorized person going through someone else's private documents has every reason to challenge that person on what he or she is doing there. That simple question applied in each life a dozen times a week will reveal if there are places and habits that are not in keeping with one's mission in life.

In the city where I was raised in India I had some very close friends. When we entered our teen years there came a time when we were all faced with the challenge of making a serious commitment to Christ. Some did, and some did not. Yet others chose to straddle two worlds. As the years went by, our lives separated in different directions, and I had settled in the United States. Many years later I was visiting my home city, and the mother of one of the young women we used to know, who had made the choice to live in two worlds, asked if I would come to her home and visit her daughter. I was informed that she was in a very sorry state, lying in bed almost as a vegetable from an attempt to take her own life.

I was not prepared for what I would encounter. I arrived at the home and was greeted by the mother, who immediately ushered me into the room of this young woman. I had not seen her in more than twenty years. As I stared at her fragile, emaciated frame, my heart sank. She was being fed intravenously and needed a nurse constantly by her side. She had been in that condition for over a year. My mind was flooded with memories from happier days we had once enjoyed. Whether she could hear I do not know, but when I called her by name she became very agitated as she struggled and uttered some incomprehensible sounds that were more like grunts and gurgles than anything else. She was indeed a pitiful sight. Deep within me was the question, "What happened? Why are you in this condition?"

On the surface the answer was straightforward. She and her mother had an argument, and in an uncontrolled fit of rage she locked herself in a bathroom and took an overdose of medication. A long while later, her mother recognized that something was wrong and forced the door open only to find her daughter unconscious. She was rushed to the hospital, but this was all that was rescued of her. Now left to live with the fallout of that impulsive act were her confused children, a devastated husband, a guilt-ridden mother, and heartbroken friends.

One can fully sympathize that unfortunate clashes of will do occur in life. Evidently some temperaments react with such impulsiveness to any conflict. But was a dispute or disappointment so insurmountable that she should forget those who needed her love and cherished her life? Was life so disposable that it could be destroyed over an argument? Somewhere in the decision-making process she had come adrift from a clear purpose for living, and the wasted body bespoke a lost or at least a distraught spirit. A life so precious to God now lay as a shadow of humanity, and death must have seemed very welcome.

Purpose! That all-important peg on which the rest of life hangs. How costly an error when that peg has no anchor. Sometimes one's entire future is determined in one momentary lapse. Tens of thousands of young people could save themselves a lifetime of remorse if they understood how a few minutes can influence or shape the future. The game of North American football is often called a game of inches. Life itself is molded and played out sometimes in seconds. With such limitless possibilities, the principle must be etched in our consiousnesses: **Anything that refreshes you without diminishing you, distracting you, or destroying the ultimate goal is a legitimate pleasure in life.**

Illicit Pleasure

There is a second principle Boreham gives to us, which has been gleaned from 2 Samuel 23. The passage is a vaguely familiar one and describes an occasion when David, embattled by the Philistines, was hiding at a cave in Adullam. One sultry night, thinking about the comforts of home, he let escape from his lips a simple longing, indeed, a very innocent longing—a wish for a drink from a certain well in Bethlehem. But it was a pleasure that could not be fulfilled, because a Philistine garrison was stationed at Bethlehem.

Hearing his sigh, three of David's mightiest soldiers, out of their love for him, found a way and made a plan. In a cloak-and-dagger operation that risked their own lives, they slipped behind the Philistine garrison, managed to get some water from the well, and returned safely, bearing that surprise gift to David.

One can only imagine David's expression when he received this gift. He was quite overwhelmed by their devotion to him and by their willingness to sacrifice their own lives to get him his wish. He raised the water to his lips, and then, before he could drink it, he slowly lowered it again and poured it onto the ground. "Far be it from me, O LORD, to do this! . . . Is it not the blood of men who went at the risk of their lives?" (2 Sam. 23:17). With those words he denied himself that pleasure.

David's action is very laudable. He felt that his own self-fulfillment in a need that was so temporary could not be justified by putting at risk the life of another. This gives us our second principle: **Any pleasure that jeopardizes the sacred right of another is an illicit pleasure.**

But let us pause lest we miss the monumental implication of a simple principle such as this. Had David kept the same caution in mind years before when he set eyes upon Bathsheba, all of Old Testament history could have been different. He knew when he brought her into his palace that he was robbing Uriah of his sacred privilege to have his wife unto himself. That impulsive act ultimately led to murder and to untold tragedy.

The first time I struck upon this principle I recall feeling a great sense of confidence and relief that it would be easy to spot a mistake such as this and therefore to guard against it. Why would anyone want to deny someone else his or her sacred right? But the more I reflected, the subtle nature of this pitfall loomed larger than I had ever thought. The personal application struck home when I read about an incident that at first seemed hard to believe. The story was told by Rich

Wilkerson, who had just finished speaking at a junior high school assembly when the principal approached one of Wilkerson's friends and told him this story.

He said that the previous year they had an eighth grade student in the school whose situation brought much grief to the school community. All of a sudden and for no apparent reason, this thirteen-year-old boy had started coming to school one hour late every day.

"I couldn't get this boy to come to school on time. First, I sent notes to his parents. He would bring the note back the next day signed by his parents—an hour late!" the principal said. "Second, I paddled the young man. The next day he showed up at school—an hour late." No matter what disciplinary method the school administrators tried, the following day the boy would still come an hour late. Finally they suspended him for a few days. His first day back at school he returned—an hour late.

"I just couldn't take it anymore, so the next day I contacted the department of welfare. The welfare agents accompanied me to the boy's home. We walked up to the front door and knocked. No one answered. So I turned the doorknob. It was open, so we walked in, and what we found wasn't very pretty. We were to discover that two months earlier, while he was at school, the boy's parents had left home." They had left a large supply of groceries in the cupboards and refrigerator, but they themselves were gone. The boy had no idea where they were. He felt abandoned and betrayed, ashamed to tell the story to the school authorities. So every day he would get his eight-year-old sister and six-year-old brother out of bed, bathe and dress them for school, and then walk them to their elementary school two miles away. Try as he might, he could never run fast enough to get to his own school earlier than one hour late.[7]

The Subtle Betrayal

The question was on the surface—how can anyone be so irresponsible and cruel? But then I began to feel some personal discomfort. No, of course an average person would never be so heartless as to inflict such deprivation upon his or her own children. But irresponsibility does not only come in the form of such a harsh choice. Often ignoring our children for personal gain or personal ambition strikes in a more sophisticated and subtle form.

Listen, for example, to the words of Doctors Minirth and Meier as they explain the high rate of depression among high-performers and the web of self-centered choices that lie beneath the surface.

> Out of all the various personality types in our culture, there is one type that is more likely than any other to get depressed at some time in life. That type is the "nice guy"—the person who is self-sacrificing, overly conscientious, over-dutiful, hard-working, and frequently quite religious. Psychiatrists call this type the obsessive-compulsive personality. Most lay persons call him a perfectionist, or a "workaholic," or even a dedicated servant. . . . Many find this quite surprising. . . . But those who have made a study of the depth of unconscious human dynamics realize that is really quite fair. . . . Those dedicated servants who get depressed have as many struggles with personal selfishness as the parasite on welfare, but the selfishness of the perfectionist is much more subtle. While he is out in society serving humanity at a work pace of eighty to a hundred hours a week, he is selfishly ignoring his wife and children. . . . In his own eyes, and in the eyes of society, he is the epitome of human dedication . . . while his wife suffers from loneliness . . . and his sons . . . eventually commit suicide. . . . He becomes angry when his wife and children place demands on him. He can't understand how they could have the nerve to call such an unselfish, dedicated servant a selfish husband and father. . . . In reality, his wife and children are correct, and they are suffering severely because of this subtle selfishness. This is precisely the reason why so many of the children of pastors, missionaries, and doctors turn out to be rebellious.[8]

Is this overstated? For some that may be so, but I strongly suspect that the truth is very discomforting here. Looking at my own life from that angle was not easy. The irresponsibility and the appalling tragedy of those three children abandoned for months by their parents is all too easy to recognize. But the surrender to a lifestyle that deprives our children on a regular basis of the time they need with us is not so easy to spot until the years have gone by.

Planes to catch. Meetings to keep. Sermons to prepare. All are well-intentioned. But then the special days come and go, and you realize some very treasured opportunities have gone. Yet the pace of life and travel have led so many busy people to give greater attention to machines and to jobs and to corporations than to the young lives that have been entrusted to their care, who long for some time with them.

If we are to keep our children from being devoured by the ever-increasing pleasures of this-worldliness, then we had better learn to deny ourselves the selfish pleasures of being consumed by our jobs at the cost of our families. **Any pleasure that jeopardizes the sacred right of another is an illicit pleasure.**

The Key Ingredient

This brings us to the third principle, which is found in Proverbs 25:16. The verse itself, in our culture, would not win an award for aesthetic elegance, but the truth is stated as forthrightly as one might want: "If you find honey, eat just enough. Too much of it, and you will vomit." The principle is obvious: **Any pleasure, however good, if not kept in balance, will distort reality or destroy appetite.**

As pleasure provides options for us, first and foremost let us make sure it is "honey," meaning it is something good and not harmful. But one cannot stop there. Even that which is good, if not kept in balance, will bring either obsession or monotony and ultimately lessen the pleasure. Few activities are as enriching to me as times of reading and relaxation, but that does not mean I should spend twenty-four hours of the day in turning pages and resting. The same applies even to an activity as important as a time of prayer and study of the Scriptures. Life must have balance to keep all of reality in view, not just one facet of it. The festivals God instituted for His people purposefully distributed the focus of the truth that needed their attention. At times it was their redemption they were to celebrate. At other times they were to remember God's faithfulness throughout their history. There were times to remember the pain that they had survived and other times for the harvest they had just received.

We have heard it said that variety is the spice of life. But it is not so much the *spice* of life as much as it is life itself, and only he or she who knows how to reach out to that bounteous variety can truly enjoy the riches of a God of abundance.

Charles Haddon Spurgeon told of a time he sat frustrated for hours, trying to arrive at a suitable sermon for his Sunday service. It was one of those efforts that seemed to come to nought no matter what he tried. Deciding to go for a walk, he came to a bench in a garden encircled by a cemetery and sat down for a rest. As he watched people come and go he noticed that the approaches into that garden were very different. There was one well-paved road. Another was a winding path. A third was a walkway that was unpaved but covered with varying sizes of stone. He noticed that all of the paths were well used—and found a title for his sermon: "Gathering at the Center." He portrayed life's journey for each of us. Some of us find ourselves walking over the solid path laid by someone else's hard efforts. For others it may have been through the winding vicissitudes of various circumstances that we have traveled. A third group struggles over bumps and dips but somehow makes it. And all gather at the center.

This is a beautiful picture illustrating that all of us come from such different backgrounds, privileges, and responsibilities. We can be sure that the same delights do not enthrall all of us in the same way. For one a beautiful symphony may be a balm for the heart's wounds. For another an energetic sporting event may provide respite. For a third, a conversation on a great theme may put iron into the blood. Whatever it may be, so long as it meets the test of God's purpose for your life, is not enjoyed at the expense of another, and provides the opportunity to lead a life that is balanced, we shall all gather at the center where God Himself is sufficient pleasure for all of the heart's longings.

LESSONS FOR THE WISE

On the basis of these three principles, there follow three very profound applications. The first is that **all pleasure must be bought at a price.** For true pleasure the price is paid before it is enjoyed. For false pleasure the price is paid after it is enjoyed.

Turning aside from immediate gratification is one of the most difficult things to do. But this is where the battle is often won or lost. In blunt terms we are called upon to be strong in our wills at resisting illicit pleasures. As a rule, many have so surrendered their wills to a state of weaknesses that they have lost sight of their capacity for strength. It is far better, goes the old adage, to shun the bait than to struggle in the snare. Learn to say "no" and to mean it—not just for the sake of saying no but because life has been defined for its ultimate purpose. If we do not resist and instead go the easy way of succumbing, there will be a price to be paid someday.

During the Vietnam war, one of its heroes was an American soldier by the name of Lance Sijan. Today, a dormitory at the Air Force Academy in Colorado is named after him. Author Malcolm McDonnell tells his story in the book *Into the Mouth of the Cat.* On November 9, 1967, Sijan was flying an F-4 on his fifty-third combat mission when, owing to a faulty fuse that triggered an explosion in his aircraft, he crashed on the border of Laos. He could have been rescued as his comrades flew near, looking for him. But he lay low and did not draw them to his spot, because the enemy was too close and he did not want his compatriots to risk their lives. Over the next forty-six days, he crawled three miles. He tried to survive on leaves and the bark of trees. Finally caught and put into solitary confinement, he was tortured to extract secrets. Those who could overhear what was happening ached for him deeply but were proud beyond measure at his unbreakable will and his determination not to betray his trust. There was nothing his tormentors could do to dent his courage and his commitment to his country. Such is the material of which true heroes are made.

If it is possible for men and women to serve their country with such unyielding honor, can we not also serve the Lord our God with a will that resists fleeting and illicit pleasures? In fact, in the thirty-fifth chapter of Jeremiah God raises this very question. He asks His people to take note of the discipline some show to earthly causes. How much more ought we to be unflinching in our commitment to God Himself. The well-known radio talk-show counselor Laura Schlesinger, responding to a male caller who claimed he had an addiction to a certain lifestyle, bluntly restated his problem. "It's not an addiction problem you have," she told him. "It is a character problem."

None of us likes to hear that, but it is the strength of our will to serve Him that reveals the character we possess. It is the strength of the will that will determine when the price is paid.

Contrast, for example, the lives of two men, both of whom started as pleasure fiends. The difference is that one continued in the same way even though constantly stalked by despair while the other broke the stranglehold of pleasure and found his greater fulfillment in knowing Christ. The first is the French author Guy de Maupassant. He was one of the greatest writers of short stories yet became an utterly tragic figure. Within ten years he rose from obscurity to fame. His material possessions bespoke a life of affluence—a yacht in the Mediterranean, a large house on the Norman Coast, a luxurious flat in Paris.

It was said of him that critics praised him, men admired him, and women worshiped him. Yet at the height of his fame he went insane, a condition brought on, many believe, by a sexually transmitted disease. On New Year's Day in 1892, he tried to cut his throat with a letter opener, and he lived out the last weeks of his life in a private asylum on the French Riviera. After weeks and months of mindless utterances and debilitating pain, he died at the age of forty-two. De Maupassant penned his own epitaph: "I have coveted everything and taken pleasure in nothing."

The destruction of such a life is an incalculable loss. It is not just that a life has gone wrong, but that the life of a genius has been so mangled and cut short. That same artistic skill and power of story-writing could have brought hours of legitimate pleasure for generations to come, yet it was suffocated because of a mind that failed to pay the price of resistance to pleasure that was illicit. Both the lack of an ultimate purpose for his life and his willingness to jeopardize others made his own life a short story, a tragedy at that.

By contrast, a writer of more recent vintage was on a similar road of confusion and aimlessness; his biography is a sordid tale. In his own words, he has subtitled his life as a "Chronicle of Wasted Years." He too was pleasure driven, at times to the bizarre. But the splendor of Christ finally won him over. He is Malcolm Muggeridge, one of England's most articulate journalists, and this is how he summed up his pursuit of pleasure.

> I may, I suppose, regard myself, or pass for being, as a relatively successful man. People occasionally stare at me in the streets—that's fame. I can fairly easily earn enough to qualify for admission to the higher slopes of the Internal Revenue—that's success. Furnished with money and a little fame even the elderly, if they care to, may partake of trendy diversions—that's pleasure. It might happen once in a while that something I said or wrote was sufficiently heeded for me to persuade myself that it represented a serious impact on our time—that's fulfillment. Yet I say to you—and I beg you to believe me—multiply these tiny triumphs by a million, add them all together, and they are nothing—less than nothing, a positive impediment—measured against one draught of that living water Christ offers to the spiritually thirsty, irrespective of who or what they are.[9]

Everything else is an impediment when measured against one draught of that living water. Those are the words of one who tasted from both offerings—the contrasting pleasures of the world and the person of Christ.

THE JOY OF IT ALL

That leads to the second application, which is the inescapable reality that we as human beings have. The Scriptures tell us of Jesus' goal as He faced the cross—"Who for the joy set before him endured the cross, scorning its shame, and sat down at the right hand of the throne hand of God" (Heb. 12:2). Joy is by far the greater goal in life. So the application is this: **Pleasure is a means, not an end. Joy should be the greater end.**

Joy is the fulfillment that comes from a relationship that breathes contentment in being and is not dependent on just doing. That kind of attitude in life finds rest in the ordinary without the restlessness that awaits the extraordinary. That is why, when pleasure has gone, it either leaves behind honor or dishonor, joy or sorrow. But life joyfully lived lives beyond pleasure or pain and is anchored in the security of the one who even enables us to exult in the commonplace things of life.

Our personal search is for that which is internal and spiritual, which in turn gives meaning to the routine, not just to the sporadic breaks from the routine to the highly charged moments. Most pleasure, if it ignores the spirit but satisfies the body, will leave behind a nagging doubt whether the experienced pleasure was right or wrong. When it is wrong, you are robbed of the joy God gives to His children. Every pleasure that is sought as an end in itself ultimately ceases to satisfy, and the hunger for a joy that rises above everything else continues.

At various stages of our lives the need for pleasure seems to be satisfied by different means. A child may find contentment in his or her small world of toys and stories, but the little one still needs the joy of its mother's presence. The very nursing of that child, of clasping the infant in a life-giving and life-receiving embrace to give it sustenance from the mother's body, is a portrait of fulfillment for both. The joy felt and received is almost sacred.

A young person finds that repose in romance and sometimes in friendships. Again there is the longing for the touch, the feel, the presence of another. A young adult pursues that complete fulfillment into marriage, one of the most joyful unions in life. An older man or woman may look beyond that stage to the treasured embrace of the family or the spouse whom age has also ravaged but whose presence is invaluable. Psychologists are reminding us of what the loss of a loved one does to the heart, even in the most cerebrally driven person. When a cherished person dies something within the surviving person dies, too.

If we were to look carefully at which pleasures bring joy and which pleasures diminish it, we would discover that every genuine and enduring pleasure is tied somehow into a relationship that also has a moral commitment. Where a relationship is immoral, pleasure comes unhinged from honor and eventually withers. Solomon's relationships became detached from commitment, and people became things of gratification. No one ought to be so denuded. A person is not a means to pleasure but an entity to whom honor is due. All relationships must recognize the supreme value of personhood.

But these relationships too are pointers. Their joys will dim or be broken if they are not nourished by and do not point to the greatest relationship of all, with God Himself. In short, the older we get the more it takes to fulfill the longing of our hearts for joy unspeakable. And only God is big enough for that.

But here let us take note of how God describes that relationship. It is an *indwelling.* Paul talked of "Christ *in* you, the hope of glory" (Col. 1:27, emphasis added). This is the ultimate intermeshing of two entities in a relationship with God. The longing for a lasting pleasure is finally and fully satisfied, for God who is spirit comes and makes His dwelling place in the spirit of the individual. No pleasure in the world can match that. This is pure joy.

For those who do not know this inner presence or in whom the spiritual has been neglected or ignored, this kind of joy is incomprehensible. C. S. Lewis once said, "How little people know who think holiness is dull." It is not possible to explain the consummation of marital love to a child when it has no concept of marital love or, at that stage, even the capacity to understand it. When the capacity is gained but the opportunity for expression is stifled, the longing increases while the fulfillment awaits.

In the same way, the unspiritual person does not even have the concept of spiritual fulfillment, and he or she pursues poor substitutes in pleasure, with diminishing returns. But the spiritually minded person wins in the double sense of pleasure's best, which is joy. In the first instance, that indwelling Christ enriches life beyond measure by fusing our spirits with His enduring joy. But even at that, the one so indwelled knows that at present the joy is expressed within physical and earthly terms and the final experience of joy is awaiting us in heaven in an eternal state. That is the joy that is set before us when both the capacity for sacred pleasure and the opportunity for its complete expression converge in the embrace of God.

In rare moments we get a brief glimpse of what that heavenly joy will be. There is a magnificent old song that speaks of this:

> Seated one day at the organ
> I was weary and ill at ease,
> And my fingers wandered idly
> over the noisy keys.
> I know not what I was playing,
> or what I was dreaming then,
> But I struck one chord of music
> Like the sound of a great Amen.
>
> It flooded the crimson twilight
> like the close of an angel's psalm,
> And it lay on my fevered spirit
> like the touch of infinite calm.
> It quieted pain and sorrow,
> like love overcoming strife.
> It seemed a harmonious echo
> from our discordant life.

It linked all perplexed meanings
into one perfect peace,
And it trembled away into silence
as if it were loathe to cease.

I have sought, but I seek it vainly—
that one lost chord divine
Which came from the soul of the organ
and entered into mine.

It may be that Death's bright angel
Will speak in that chord again,
It may be that only in heav'n
I shall hear that grand Amen.
It may be that Death's bright angel
will speak in that chord again—
It may be that only in heav'n
I shall hear that grand Amen.[10]

The psalmist says in Psalm 16:11, "You have made known to me the path of life; you will fill me with joy in your presence, with eternal pleasures at your right hand." What does he mean, "joy in your presence and pleasure at your right hand"? How best can I understand that now?

Years ago, I finished reading what I consider one of the finest books of this century, G. K. Chesterton's *Orthodoxy.* Unfortunately, I do not agree with some of the writer's theology. But when writing to the skeptic, his arguments for the Christian life are breathtaking. He talks about this thing we call joy in knowing Christ. He points out that for the Christian, joy is central and sorrow is peripheral. That is because life's fundamental questions are answered and only the peripheral ones are not. But for the one who does not know Christ, sorrow is central and joy peripheral, because the peripheral questions may be answered but the fundamental ones are not. As he brings that book to a close, he raises a profound question. Why, he wonders, does the Bible never mention anything that describes laughter in the life of Christ? We hear of Him weeping, angry, moved with compassion, and in a host of other sentiments. But we do not ever read "and Jesus laughed." Only Chesterton would have dared to raise the question, for he had a rare gift of sanctified imagination, which he would need in attempting an answer. I think it is brilliant.

> Joy, which was the small publicity of the pagan, is the gigantic secret of the Christian. And as I close this chaotic volume I open again the strange small book from which all Christianity came; and I am again haunted by a kind of confirmation. The tremendous figure which fills the Gospels towers in this respect, as in every other, above all the thinkers who ever thought themselves tall. His pathos was natural, almost casual. The Stoics, ancient and modern, were proud of concealing their tears. He never concealed His tears; He showed them plainly on His open face at any daily sight, such as the far sight of His native city. Yet He concealed something. Solemn supermen and imperial diplomatists are proud of restraining their anger. He never restrained His anger. He flung furniture down the front steps of the Temple, and asked men how they expected to escape the damnation of Hell. Yet He restrained something. I say it with reverence; there was in that shattering personality a thread that must be called shyness. There was something that He hid from all men when He went up a mountain to pray. There was something that He covered constantly by abrupt silence or impetuous isolation. There was some one thing that was too great for God to show us when He walked upon our earth; and I have sometimes fancied that it was His mirth.[11]

What mirth that must be! Chesterton may be right. There is no analogy in the present for ultimate joy and eternal pleasure. The best of our pleasures only hint at what awaits us. That begins with the very indwelling of Christ within us, that ecstasy the world does not know.

STAYING CLOSE TO THE SOURCE

This brings us to the final application: **God is the source of all good pleasure.** In fact, the closer one gets to legitimate pleasure, the closer one gets to the heart of God. C. S. Lewis gave us this perceptive intimation in his book *The Screwtape Letters.* The senior devil has instructed the junior devil on how to trip up an individual who seems to be straddling the line between God and self. "Keep him from going over to the Enemy," was the charge given to the young imp. Some days later the junior devil returned to the senior devil and reported that he had lost the man over completely to "the Enemy's" side, meaning that the individual had made his commitment to God.

"How did that happen?" roared the senior devil. "Could you not have seduced him?"

"No," came the reply, "because he did two things that took him away from us. First, everyday he took a walk, not for the exercise but for the pure pleasure of it. Second, he decided to read a good book, not so that he might quote it to someone else, but rather, for the pure pleasure of it. Between the walk and the good book, he came within the Enemy's reach."[12]

This is a thrilling insight from Lewis. We have become so conditioned to a morbid interpretation of the Christian life that we have robbed ourselves of the sheer delights and pleasures that God has made possible for us. The closer we get to legitimate pleasures, the closer we move into His voice and grasp. The closer we get to illicit pleasures, the further we get from His reach. As we lay hold of the principles that bring us close to Him His voice becomes clearer and the intimacy becomes richer. Just as all truth is God's truth, so is all legitimate pleasure a gift from God. Receive it with thanks and draw near to Him as a result.

A POSTSCRIPT

To sum up this great theme of pleasure, there is left but one thing to say. The Bible tells us much about the pleasure that comes to us from serving God. But it also reminds us of the supreme compliment that God has paid us. In His sovereign plan and grace, He has made us such that in our service of Him we bring to God *His* greatest pleasure. In Psalm 147:11 we are reminded that "the LORD delights in those who fear him, who put their hope in his unfailing love."

His pleasure and ours will meet consummately when we receive the divine accolade, "Well done, good and faithful servant." In those words will be locked up the purpose for which God has made us. That goal must govern the pleasure of our lives: to hear Him say, "Well done." No other words will bring the heart such ultimate joy as those words for which we long. How that is best foreshadowed and lived out in this world, I have saved for the final chapter.

Six

The Cry of a Lonely Heart

NOVELIST AND WRITER Thomas Wolfe, having himself lived an emotionally turbulent life, articulated one of the most deeply felt aches within the human heart:

> The whole conviction of my life now rests upon the belief that loneliness, far from being a rare and curious phenomenon, peculiar to myself and to a few other solitary people, is the central and inevitable feature of human existence.
>
> All this hideous doubt, despair and dark confusion of the soul a lonely man must know, for he is united to no image save that which he creates himself. He is bolstered by no other knowledge save that which he can gather for himself with the vision of his own eyes and brain. He is sustained and cheered and aided by no party. He is given comfort by no creed. He has no faith in him except his own, and often that faith deserts him, leaving him shaken and filled with impotence. Then it seems to him that his life has come to nothing. That he is ruined, lost, and broken, past redemption, and that morning, that bright and shining morning

> with its promise of new beginnings, will never come upon the earth again as it did once.[1]

Along a similar vein, D. H. Lawrence sounded a somber postscript to his own pursuit for happiness—but he added an important twist that forces the reader to think long and hard before surrendering to his conclusion:

> We want to delude ourselves that of the problem of our emptiness, love is at the root. I want to say to you, it isn't. Love is only the branches. The root goes beyond love. A naked kind of isolation. An isolated me that does not meet and mingle and never can. It is true what I say. There is a beyond in me which goes further than love, beyond the scope of stars. Just as some stars are beyond the scope of our vision, so our own search goes beyond the scope of love. At least, I think that it is at the root, going beyond love itself.[2]

A REALITY THAT HAUNTS

Have these two authors touched the throbbing nerve of a reality that holds all of us in its grip? Are they telling it as it really is? Or is this just literary license in the hands of melodramatic and eccentric artists?

Tempting though it might be for the optimist to dismiss these words as cynically spoken in some dark moment of despair, there are many who would echo the same feeling of desolation. I would venture to say that this cry is felt by all, though better suppressed by some. As one actress recently quipped, "We are all in this together alone."

I believe that Wolfe and Lawrence are right. Our experience of loneliness is universal, and love alone is not the answer. There *is* a "beyond" in all of us that love does not satisfy. As wonderful a privilege as love is, I strongly suspect that even in its best form we have made of it something it was never meant to be. While the pervert chases after the physical only to come away ever unsatiated, the purist exalts love to emotional expectations that it could never deliver on a sustained basis.

This was the very indictment author Denis de Rougemonts had in mind when he said that love ceases to be a demon only when it ceases to be a god. In other words, love becomes a scourge when it is idolized as an end in itself. Yet we still pursue it like a hunter and assume that "that thing called love" is our final trophy, exalting it in our songs and talking of it in platitudes that it can never equal. As grand an experience as love is, it is not the final answer to loneliness. The heart, like a probing device, worms and bends its way through obstacles and opportunities, ever exploring deeper to find a nestling place—looking for that beyond.

From the one-liners on the T-shirts worn by Generation Xers crying out to be heard to the sentimental movies of a by-gone era, tales of love and passion litter the landscape. Sometimes they provide an escape; at other times they create a hunger. The search for the beyond goes on inexorably and unabated. In a sense, this continuing restlessness is not just disconcerting but devastating to our modern and postmodern egos. After all, every facility accorded to us to bring more companionship has only been increased or improved with time.

Yet in a puzzling manner the more we have access to, the further we seem to be from finding the answer to loneliness. The best analogy one can find is that of a young boy surrounded by the most sophisticated and expensive gifts at Christmas time. Minutes after the gifts have been unwrapped he sits staring at the wall, depressed by exhausting so much in so little time. In a similar manner, having tasted of every new offering and experience that has come along, we wonder with puzzlement where all the promised fulfillment has disappeared.

In our current socioeconomic scene, at least four great gains have been made, all of which were welcomed with the promise they brought of a new day. Yet disappointment has accompanied these advances. First and foremost, this is the age of communication. Never before have we had such means to instantly transmit content or create desire.

The incredible has actually happened when even men have taken to letter-writing because it has been wedded to machines and ingeniously captioned E-mail. (Had it just been mail its allurement would have been lost. The "E" before the "mail" has endowed it with technological respectability.) Yet in the midst of all our communication capacities the walls between races and cultures and generations have become higher and more difficult to climb. I have on numerous occasions heard parents complain of a son or a daughter who sits alone in front of a computer all evening long, silent and distant from the rest of the family.

Sensitivities between people are still high: Baby boomers. Baby Busters. Generation X. Heaven knows what new title awaits the inheritors of what is left. Lines are drawn by social theorists, and where none seem apparent, marketing geniuses step in to create new lines.

Second, the age of technology has delivered a bill of goods for which the cost is exacted more in the loss of our peace of mind than in our bank accounts. Each new invention was supposed to save us time. Yet when a traveler arrives in cities such as Hong Kong or Singapore, these bastions of technological gadgetry and economic strength, it becomes quickly obvious that even there the lights at the office are burning deep into the night. Just one more deal must be struck, just one more competitor must be bested, because it is no longer every day that counts but every second. Delay can mean bankruptcy.

In an age when conveniences were intended to free up time for leisure, actually less time is spent in building relationships while more time is invested in using those conveniences. The immediacy thrust upon men and women who are making huge corporate decisions has only increased the anxiety levels. The new term for such executive living is "constant whitewater."

Third, medicine has brought us vastly improved means to preserve life, and yet we have lost the definition of life itself. Now we are talking about the right to die when we are mature and hurting without having been given the right to live when we are fragile and needy.

Every value is now redefined. Progress of means has brought with it regress in essence and understanding. C. S. Lewis wrote at one time that there was a similarity between technology and magic that separated them from the wisdom of the ages. To the ancient of old, the question was how to conform the soul to reality, and the answer was in virtue and wisdom. To the contemporary modern, the question is how to reconfigure reality so it conforms to our passions. The answer is in technique or technology.[3]

All our advances notwithstanding, never before has a generation lived so much on antacids and antidepressants in an effort to calm harried spirits, finding band-aid solutions to dislocated joints. The witch doctor with his jars of animal secretions and magical concoctions must feel flattered to have been ahead of his time.

Fourth, human sexuality has never been more studied, offered up, and pandered to in public, yet we have never been more confused about what is right or, for that matter, even normal in such expressions. One woman in England looking at a magazine intended for teenage girls was horrified to realize that the intent and extent of the magazine in its articles and pictures was to make young girls "sexually crazed." They were planting in young minds cravings that no human experience could match or placate.

With such mangling contradictions, is it any wonder that we sense an isolation and cynicism, a search for a beyond that seems ever more elusive? Increased communication capacity, technological advances, progress in medicine, and sexual liberation have, all in their own way, only made us a more captive and trivial culture. The cry of loneliness is heard from millions of hearts, and love alone is not the answer. Why, then, do we suffer the condition of loneliness, and what is the answer?

THE TIES THAT BIND

Two of the most moving stories in the New Testament will give us the clue that there is a greater pursuit in life than love. To this end I can say without reserve that the glory of womanhood provides a more readily visible aid than the sometimes devious sophistication of manhood. One of the most fascinating aspects of Jesus' teaching is to watch the difference with which He handles the emotional makeup of a woman against that of a man. For men in that day, as I am afraid it is in ours, the peril of appearing to be vulnerable was one of the greatest fears. Few men I know are willing to admit emotional need. To borrow money or to ask for endorsements—that is one thing. But to admit to a need for emotional succor or physical consolation is another matter. Our young men are overtly trained to be above that. Not so is the candor of womanhood.

Some time ago my wife and I took a train journey while we were overseas, purely to be away from the intrusions of telephones and fax machines and to be alone together for a few days. The day after we disembarked, we found ourselves at a restaurant, sharing a table with a couple who had also been on that train. I struck up a conversation with the man as my wife did with the woman.

Halfway through our conversation I looked in the direction of my wife and noticed that she was obviously comforting this other woman, for whom tears had started to flow. I had no clue of what had transpired until we were back in our room. All through the evening the man had talked about the law firm of which he was the senior partner. It was the largest law firm in his country and one of the most influential in the world. The entire conversation revolved around the success and busyness of his career.

At the same time his wife had told my wife that the only reason they were on this trip was to work through the grief of the death of their young son, some years before. "We have never really broken free of that hurt," she wept. "We have needed the time to talk about it and to face up to the tragedy."

Two different points of focus were being demonstrated for two individuals equally wounded. One never broached the subject but was willing to talk endlessly about his high-paced life in economic terms, while the other irrepressibly opened up to a stranger and spoke about the broken dreams of her life.

The encounters of Jesus with the men and women of the Bible tell a similar tale. When He addressed Nicodemus Jesus was talking to a man whose identity was proudly locked up in his rabbinical knowledge, yet he betrayed an ignorance of the most basic spiritual miracle—that of God's transforming power within the human heart. In the instance of the rich young ruler, Jesus was face to face with one for whom his wealth was the object of his worship. Dealing with his real need seemed too difficult for the young ruler to concede, and he went away sorrowful because he had wanted Jesus to endorse his primary pursuit—money.

The interactions with the two women who now briefly occupy our attention make evident to us how Jesus gently but permanently opened the wellsprings of their hearts and, in doing so, gave us two timeless object lessons. The story of the Samaritan woman is often repeated because of its real-life feel. Here was one who lived a life of quiet desperation. Listening in on her conversation as she talked to Jesus about her hope for the coming of the Messiah someday, and her puzzlement over which mountain to worship in, leaves one suspecting that her real struggle in life had not yet been broached. Jesus' disarmingly gentle triumph in getting her to admit that her pathetic state of rejection was the chief of her woes is a classic illustration of how God unmasks our facades of concerns.

But this was not done so that He could stare her in the eye and say, "Checkmate!" Looming behind her nervousness and her welter of religious questions was her greatest heartache—her loneliness. She sought a drink that would assuage her deepest thirst but did not know how close at hand that drink was. The message with which He left her is profoundly instructive indeed.

The second story is even more melodramatic. It is also one that has inspired hymn-writers over the years. The incident took place in the home of a Pharisee named Simon. The narrative clearly would have shocked both the ones in the story and the readers who would later read the story as it built toward a proverbial climax. Listen to the words of Luke:

> Now one of the Pharisees invited Jesus to have dinner with him, so he went to the Pharisee's house and reclined at the table. When

> a woman who had lived a sinful life in the town learned that Jesus was eating at the Pharisee's house, she brought an alabaster jar of perfume, and as she stood behind him at his feet weeping, she began to wet his feet with her tears. Then she wiped them with her hair, kissed them and poured perfume on them.
>
> When the Pharisee who had invited him saw this, he said to himself, "If this man were a prophet, he would know who is touching him and what kind of woman she is—that she is a sinner."
>
> Jesus answered him, "Simon, I have something to tell you."
>
> "Tell me, teacher," he said.
>
> "Two men owed money to a certain moneylender. One owed him five hundred denarii, and the other fifty. Neither of them had the money to pay him back, so he canceled the debts of both. Now which of them will love him more?"
>
> Simon replied, "I suppose the one who had the bigger debt canceled."
>
> "You have judged correctly," Jesus said. (Luke 7:36–43)

Jesus then proceeded to point out to Simon that even though He had come into his home as a guest, none of the courtesies offered a guest were accorded Him. There had been no embrace. No water to wash His feet, no towel with which to dry them. No offer was made to bring refreshment for Him after His dust-ridden journey. This woman, by contrast, had dared to come in uninvited. She had given to Jesus the best of her possessions and then fallen prostrate at His feet, washing them with her tears and drying them with her hair. Her shocking gesture and broken countenance spoke volumes of her gratitude and love and would have left all but the most arrogant speechless. Everything in that culture's book of etiquette was disregarded in that encounter of a lost woman with her newfound Savior.

Both this story and that of the woman of Samaria end on a very powerful note conveying the divine imperative for us to follow likewise. There are similar clues in both stories to the answer of the heart's struggle of loneliness and the longing for the beyond. But before we can reach that point, there is an existential journey we must take.

The Loves We Need

After years of reflection on this issue and listening to how the struggle has been verbalized across many cultures, I have found, in the writings of C. S. Lewis on the theme of love, the seed of an answer. When his book *The Four Loves* was originally published, it won critical acclaim and the recognition that Lewis had pinpointed the Achilles heel of love. However fulfilling that love may be, Lewis had ingeniously mirrored the soul of humanity in its hunger for something greater.

With typical Lewis humility, the book ended with the words, "And with this, where a better book would begin, mine must end." Unfortunately for the reader, only Lewis could have bettered his own book. But he has left us with enough ideas to spur us on further.[4]

But in his introduction, prior to expounding on the four loves, Lewis stabs at the connection between love and pleasure, wondering what binds them and what separates them. Concealed within this struggle, I believe, lies a monumental truth. It is only a preamble for him, but probed further, it can lead us to a profound conclusion.

The four concepts in that introduction begin with the assertion of a broad category he calls Need-love. Which of us does not understand this? We long for affection from the time we can reach out with our arms or utter our first word. Even modern psychology has thrown light on this. In the last few decades as scholars have probed deeper into human behavior, one of the aspects studied and debated has been in the so-called self-theories—understanding why we do what we do, which is then leveraged to understand what our needs are.

A pioneer in this field was Abraham Maslow, who is best known for his ideas on an individual's self-actualization, that is, how each one of us reaches his or her full potential. On a more popular level, Maslow is known for his "hierarchy of needs," which he offered as a scale on which we ascend to fulfilling that potential. The hierarchy he lists from birth to maturity are our physiological needs, safety needs, love needs, esteem needs, and finally the need for self-actualization.

Interestingly, Maslow went on later to distinguish these needs into two categories, some born out of a sense of deprivation and others from what he called "being motives." Our physiological and safety needs he placed as foundational, having lower motives, coming about because of a "felt deficiency." When they are not met, our behavior is accordingly affected. The higher motives of being unto self-actualization, he says, only come into play when those lower needs are met.

There are assumptions within Maslow's total framework that would not be in keeping with a Christian world-view. But those differences are not the reason for referencing his psychological theory. Rather, it is to point out a fundamental agreement between those of his school who wrestle with motivational theories and those who, like C. S. Lewis, use an existential apologetic; they start from the common ground of need that we human beings share with one another.

But there is also a very critical point of difference between biblical thought and Maslow that is all too definitive to ignore. The philosophical mistake that behaviorists make in defining our needs as human beings is in their starting point. They have their reasons for this, but the difference is there. They observe certain patterns of behavior from which they move backward to define what our essence must be rather than starting with our essence and moving forward to explain our behavior. This cardinal difference in understanding who we are results in dramatically different solutions for loneliness. If we understand how important this demarcation is we will understand why thinkers like Wolfe and Lawrence will never find an answer to the "beyond" outside of a Christian response.

A Mystery by Design

At its very core, life is a mystery in the best sense of the term—an engaging mystery, a thrilling mystery, a deliberate mystery. Every individual has a unique, splendid, and marvelous capacity. Having been brought into being by no will of his or her own, each person then proceeds to tackle that mystery right from the beginning.

In a provocative and, I believe, purposeful way, God has spared us the memory of our own birth. This, I am convinced, is because it is too grand for the mind to comprehend. At one stage Jesus said to His disciples, "I have spoken to you of earthly things and you do not believe; how then will you believe if I speak of heavenly things?" (John 3:12). So much even of the obvious eludes us; how dare we think we have comprehensively understood the subtle? This mysterious and awe-inspiring starting point of life itself (with its built-in limitation) ought to be our first clue to the mystery of the essence of life. Let us begin from there.

From the moment of conception to the moment of delivery there are incredible changes. That single fertilized ovum grows over nine months to a hundred trillion cells. The doctor delivering that child is no more conferring life upon the individual than the parents do in naming the child. The process of birth and the act of giving the child a name are a recognition that the life already exists. That name may be shared by millions of others, but the life itself is distinctively, uniquely that individual's. A single strand of human DNA would fill a thousand-volume encyclopedia comprising six hundred thousand pages with five hundred words on every page. Yet the individual marvelously transforms the information into a person and personality that is his or her own. Ask any parent who has identical twins. Even the similarity of chemical makeup does not make it possible for one to replace the other.

This is where we start. In His infinite wisdom and power, God the very author of life has granted to us that at which we must stand in awe. Author Lewis Thomas makes this comment in *Medusa and the Snail:*

> The mere existence of that cell should be one of the greatest astonishments of the earth. People ought to be walking around all day, all through their waking hours, calling to each other in endless wonderment, talking of nothing except that cell. . . . If anyone does succeed in explaining it within my lifetime I will charter a skywriting airplane, maybe a fleet of them, and send

them aloft to write one great exclamation point after another, around the whole sky, until all my money runs out.[5]

There is mystery that must hold us in awe. But there is a second factor in our uniqueness. Not only is it one of essence, it is one of coalescence. There is a unique wholeness that is indivisible. In each personality there is a convergence of components that cannot be separated, giving each one his or her personhood. F. W. Boreham brilliantly illustrated this in his essay "The Sword of Solomon."

> There is a sense, . . . in which two and two are four. . . .
>
> There is a plane—the plane of ledgers and cashbooks—on which these propositions are approximately sound. But if you rise from that plane to a loftier one, you will find at once that they are untenable. They simply will not work. Solomon proves it at the city gate. It may be true that half-a-sovereign and half-a-sovereign make a sovereign; it is obviously untrue that half-a-baby and half-a-baby make a baby. Let the sword do its deadly work; let it cleave this baby into two parts; and half-a-baby plus half-a-baby will represent but the grim and gruesome mockery of a baby. Two halves of a baby make no baby at all.
>
> On this higher plane of human sentiment and experience, the laws of mathematics collapse completely. When, for example, a man distributes his wealth among his children, he gives to each a part; but when a woman distributes her love among her children, she gives it all to each. . . . [No] man who has once fallen in love will ever be persuaded that one and one are only two. He looks at her, and he feels that one plus one would be a million. . . . [No] happy couple into the sweet shelter of whose home a little child has come will ever be convinced that two and one are only three. Life has been enriched a thousandfold by the addition of that one little life to theirs. And I am certain that no pair from whose clinging and protecting arms their treasure has been snatched will find comfort in the assurance that one from three leaves two. In the great crises of life one's faith in figures breaks down hopelessly.[6]

A person is not a quantity. Each person is an entity. The loss of these very marvels, our uniqueness and our individual wholeness, may be at the root of our misdirected hope in assuming that a safe and fulfilling love will assuage all hungers.

Why, I have often wondered, do we move to the behavioral stage, entranced by its data, and leave the volume of our origin unread? Is it because we do not wish to claim dependence on anyone, deluding ourselves into believing we are self-made? Held in the bind of our longing for love we have lost sight of the wonder of our essence behind the existence. To bypass our first stage of being and become preoccupied with the first stage of behaving results in a text of Need-love without a context of love. Indeed, those yearnings are real. Need-love is real. Whether we are born wealthy or poor, American or Asian, we have a built-in need, not just to be fed, but to be loved.

Every now and then you read of a dramatic expression of this need. But next time read carefully between the lines, and you will notice that it is not merely any love that is needed but a particular love. That particular love is built into our unique personality and the unique wholeness with which we are born.

Some months ago I received a copy of a mailing from a ministry in New York City that works with young people who are trapped in the drug scene and often caught in the hellish web of prostitution. I cannot recall when a few words from a stranger left such heaviness within my heart. Prior to the salutation the writer warned the reader that it would be difficult to believe the contents but vowed that every word of it was true. Here is the text of that letter:

> Dear Friend,
>
> She came to our front door Tuesday morning, dressed in dirty rags, holding a little aluminum paint can in her arms.
>
> From the second she stepped inside our shelter, she mystified us. Whatever she did, wherever she went, the paint can never left her hands.
>
> When Kathy sat in the crisis shelter, the can sat in her arms.

She took the can with her to the cafeteria that first morning she ate, and to bed with her that first night she slept.

When she stepped into the shower, the can was only a few feet away. When the tiny homeless girl dressed, the can rested alongside her feet.

"I'm sorry, this is mine," she told our counselors, whenever we asked her about it. "This can belongs to me."

"Do you want to tell me what's in it, Kathy?" I'd ask her. "Um, not today," she said, "not today."

When Kathy was sad or angry or hurt—which happened a lot—she took her paint can to a quiet dorm room on the 3rd floor. Many times on Tuesday and Wednesday and Thursday, I'd pass her room, and watch her rock gently back and forth, the can in her arms. Sometimes she'd talk to the paint can in low whispers.

I've been around troubled kids all my life. . . . I'm used to seeing them carry stuffed animals (some of the roughest, toughest kids at Covenant House have a stuffed animal). Every kid has something—needs something—to hold.

But a paint can? I could feel alarm bells ringing in my head.

Early this morning, I decided to "accidentally" run into her again. "Would you like to join me for breakfast?" I said. "That would be great," she said.

For a few minutes we sat in a corner of our cafeteria, talking quietly over the din of 150 ravenous homeless kids. Then I took a deep breath, and plunged into it. . . .

"Kathy, that's a really nice can. What's in it?"

For a long time, Kathy didn't answer. She rocked back and forth, her hair swaying across her shoulders. Then she looked over at me, tears in her eyes.

"It's my mother," she said.

"Oh," I said. "What do you mean, it's your mother?" I asked.

"It's my mother's ashes," she said. "I went and got them from the funeral home. See, I even asked them to put a label right here on the side. It has her name on it."

Kathy held the can up before my eyes. A little label on the side chronicled all that remained of her mother: date of birth, date of death, name. That was it. Then Kathy pulled the can close, hugged it.

"I never really knew my mother, Sister," Kathy told me. "I mean, she threw me in the garbage two days after I was born." (We checked Kathy's story. Sure enough the year Kathy was born, the New York newspapers ran a story saying that police had found a little infant girl in a dumpster . . . and yes, it was two days after Kathy was born.)

"I ended up living in a lot of foster homes, mad at my mother," Kathy said. "But then, I decided I was going to find her. I got lucky—someone knew where she was living. I went to her house."

"She wasn't there, Sister," she said. "My mother was in the hospital. She had AIDS. She was dying."

"I went to the hospital, and I got to meet her the day before she died. My mother told me she loved me, Sister," Kathy said crying. "She told me she loved me." (We double-checked Kathy's story . . . every word of it was true.)

I reached out and hugged Kathy and she cried in my arms for a long time. It was tough getting my arms around her, because she just wouldn't put the paint can down. But she didn't seem to mind. I know I didn't. . . .

I saw Kathy again, a couple of hours ago, eating dinner in our cafeteria. She made a point to come up and say hi. I made a point to give her an extra hug. . . .

I've felt like crying tonight. I can't seem to stop feeling this way. I guess this story—the whole horrible, sad, unreal mess—has gotten to me tonight.

I guess that's why I just had to write you this letter.[7]

Could there be another heart-wrenching story that expressed Need-love in more poignant terms? Kathy's cry from the garbage dump of rejection signaled both the agony and the glory of human existence. Was Kathy looking for love or was there something more? I believe it was something more. Let us leave this all-important first step for now and return to it when we are ready to pull all of the forms of love together.

THE GIFT OF LOVE

There is a flip side to Need-love, says Lewis, and that is Gift-love. This is the love that pours itself out in generosity, love, kindness, mercy, grace, and myriad other acts or thoughts of giving. Where would we all be if it were not for Gift-love that benefits the heart from the sacrifice or the gift of another? Whether it be a story from the battlefield where in the midst of human warfare noble deeds of rescue are carried out, or whether it be from the annals of sacrificial parental love as one lays down his or her life for another, we read and hear of gifts of love and recognize the charity bespoken by such acts and efforts.

There is an important point to be made here. One or two of the world's leading religions point to Gift-love as the ultimate virtue. The selfless life. The sacrificial life. This they define as the end to which all means must point. One of the ancient stories coming out of Buddhism tells of a woman who wanted to know how she could rid herself of her miseries and her bereavements. She was told by the sage to go from door to door and when she found a home where there were no worries, to ask there for a morsel of grain. She returned a long while later saying she had not found a single home that fit that description. In fact, she had become so involved in hearing of the heartaches of others that she had forgotten her own. The moral of the story is that in giving, you forget your own need.

We all recognize the glory of Gift-love and admire those who pour it out on those around them. But the religious theory that undergirds both this illustration and the concept itself falls desperately short of providing a satisfactory answer. Life is far more complicated than to be summarily epitomized as a journey to alleviate hurt. Here, too, there is more that could be said. But we grant Lewis's second category, Gift-love. We all have the need to be loved. We all have the privilege of giving the gift of love or of receiving the gift of love.

The Pleasure that Attracts

Having introduced us to the two kinds of love, Need-love and Gift-love, Lewis then introduces us to two kinds of pleasure, looking for a connection between our pleasures and our loves. The first he calls Need-pleasure, the second he calls Appreciation-pleasure. Need-pleasure, very plainly stated, is the contentment we get from some of life's simplest treats—a refreshing glass of water or settling down on a comfortable chair and enjoying a cup of tea (in my case) or whatever else it may be that brings enjoyment. This is Need-pleasure. Few realize its value more than the traveler who is miles away from the familiar and misses the customary delights of home. In his recent book *The Longing for Home* Frederick Buechner has a paragraph that makes just that point as he harks back on his childhood days. This is what he says:

> What was there about the house that made it home in a way that all other houses of my childhood never even came close to being? The permanence of it was part of the answer—the sense I had that whereas the other houses came and went, this one was always and would go on being there for us as far into the future as I could imagine, with Ellen bringing my grandmother her glass of buttermilk on a silver tray just at eleven every morning, and my grandfather going off to his downtown office and returning . . . before dinner with the evening paper under his arm and maybe something he'd bought at the bakery on the way home, and the Saturday night suppers when the cook was out and the menu, in honor of the New England half of my grandmother's background, was always mahogany—colored beans baked with salt pork and molasses, steamed Boston brown bread with raisins in it, and strong black coffee boiled in a pot with an eggshell to settle the

> grounds and sweetened with lumps of sugar and cream heavy enough to whip.[8]

This would be a very painful passage to read if one were hungry! But this is a classic expression of Need-pleasure. Each enjoyment of it goes into the memory bank to be drawn upon when the opportunity comes to enjoy it at some other appropriate moment.

Lewis then takes us to the final component in this quadrant of his thought. He calls it Appreciation-pleasure. This is the pleasure that comes oh! so suddenly but leaves us enthralled in its wake. One may be driving along a highway when, quite unexpectedly, around a bend in the road a field full of corn or poppies comes into view, and the spectacle is awe-inspiring. "How beautiful!" "How lovely!" seem understatements for the enjoyment received, and any description of that momentary bliss seems almost impossible. The brief flash of pleasure leaves us with both a longing and a lasting memory.

Need-love, Gift-love; Need-pleasure, Appreciation-pleasure. These are the loves and pleasures with which we live. The more they sprinkle our lives, the greater the certainty of enjoyment in living. But now a question surfaces as you put it all together. By needing and giving love, finding pleasure and appreciating pleasure, can we find the answer to loneliness? Is there a completeness in these four components? Is there a something complementary about those four experiences? Or is something still missing?

A Surprising Gap

Lewis rightly senses that there is an uneven balance between love and pleasure. Need-pleasure, he suggests, foreshadows and points us to Need-love. A refreshing glass of cold water on a hot day brings us pleasure. But that Need-pleasure is only a small seed compared to the full bloom of pleasure one finds in the arms of a loved one. When we need the love of someone and find that love requited, a unique pleasure results. So there is a connection between Need-love and

Need-pleasure. Need-love and Need-pleasure go hand in hand, even as life changes.

But does Appreciation-pleasure foreshadow Gift-love in the same way that Need-pleasure foreshadows Need-love? Something breaks down in this connection. It is easy to see the relationship between Need-pleasure and Need-love. But the connection between Appreciation-pleasure and Gift-love is not as easy to make. Appreciation-pleasure by itself falls short for at least two reasons.

First, it does not fully express our response to the gifts of love that come our way. Second, Appreciation-pleasure is a response, not only to a gift of love, but also to things like beauty and goodness, and it responds with wonder, awe, and enthrallment. When we appreciate a beautiful piece of music we want to respond in some way. We bask in the glory of a sight or a sound or a feeling that cannot be bottled up. Somehow to say that Appreciation-pleasure fully describes our state of mind in that situation seems inadequate.

I remember on one occasion being at Cape Point in South Africa. Standing at the tip of the triangle at Land's End, that vast open body of water that had tested the best of the early explorers reached as far as the eye could see. From one side surged the Atlantic Ocean and from the other side the Indian Ocean. As the two oceans met, swirling with an awesome force, we looked literally into the wild blue yonder. The sight was breathtaking. As my colleague and I watched the magnificence in silence, there was an overwhelming desire to respond in some way. But how? What can Appreciation-pleasure do? We certainly did not stop to hug a mountain near us; nor did we leave a gift at the bottom of a rock configuration or kiss the water. Appreciation-pleasure comes to a dead end and is stifled within itself.

How then does Gift-love fit in with Appreciation-pleasure? How does beauty connect to Appreciation-pleasure that needs to respond but cannot? Lewis completely understands this stifling thrill. There has to be something more, a fifth concept that would solve this dilemma. He calls it simply Appreciative love. And with this irrepressible affection he finally opens up the package that hitherto was still sealed. Now we can answer why there is a love that is deeper than our normal use of the word, even at its best. This is the way Lewis puts it:

> In the Appreciation-pleasures, even at their lowest, and more and more as they grow up into the full appreciation of all beauty, we get something that we can hardly help calling love. . . . It is the feeling which would make a man unwilling to deface a great picture even if he were the last man left alive and himself about to die; which makes us glad of unspoiled forests that we shall never see; which makes us anxious that the garden or bean-field should continue to exist. We do not merely like the things; we pronounce them, in a momentarily God-like sense, "very good."

This is when the heart and mind respond with a love that goes beyond pleasure. This is a life-enriching blend of heart and will, the coalescing of love and gratitude. But to what? Or to whom?

> It has revealed to me a deficiency in our previous classification of the loves into those of Need and those of Gift. There is a third element in love which is no less important than these, which is foreshadowed by our Appreciation-pleasures. This judgement that the object is very good, this attention (almost homage) offered to it as a kind of debt, this wish that it should be and should continue being what it is if even we were never to enjoy it, can go out not only to things but to persons. When it is offered to a woman we call it admiration; when to a man, hero-worship; when to God, worship simply.

Lewis, I am afraid, possibly out of humility, clearly underestimates the full weight of what he has said here. To introduce the concept of Appreciative love by saying that it is no less important than Need-love and Gift-love is to put them on an equal level, when in fact, Appreciative love rightly understood undergirds, influences, and informs all the others. His climactic passage on this is utterly brilliant, and from it I will build my case.

> Need-love cries to God from our poverty; Gift-love longs to serve, or even to suffer for, God; Appreciative love says: "We give thanks to thee for thy great glory." Need-love says of a woman "I cannot live without her"; Gift-love longs to give her happiness, comfort, protection—if possible, wealth; Appreciative love gazes and holds its breath and is silent, rejoices that such a wonder should exist even if not for him, will not be wholly dejected by losing her, would rather have it so than never to have seen her at all.[9]

In short, Appreciative love endures because it is rooted in the very source of our being, not merely in our behaving. We do not hug the mountain, but we can pause and say thank you to the one who made it and love Him with all of our hearts. There is a fusing of love with gratitude in such a transcending order of human relations that it can only be called worship.

G. K. Chesterton said something to the effect that if my child has Santa Claus to thank for putting candy in his stocking, have I got nobody to thank for putting two feet in mine? That is it. This is not just Appreciation-pleasure; this is Appreciative love. "Thank you" is indispensable to the highest form of love. It may be the reason that just as our celebration in North America of the festival of Thanksgiving is being renamed Turkey Day, a culture of thanklessness has given birth to a lonely generation.

This I believe to be the cornerstone of the answer to loneliness. Appreciative love springs forth out of gratitude and takes into full cognizance the mystery of my being before the one who is the cause of my being and who Himself can never, not be. Appreciative love, as it relates to our response to God, is a love that loves out of gratitude to Him; it is a love that bends the heart and will in worship. That is the "beyond" in our lives.

I have a dear friend who is a renowned preacher. Now in his early sixties, he was given up by his parents as a newborn, for some very personal reasons. Over all these years he wondered if he would ever find his parents and meet them. A few years ago, after working tirelessly, he was able to locate his mother. She is obviously in her senior years, and when he made contact and asked if he could come and visit her, her heart overflowed with a joy she could not contain. This was a pleasure she had thought she would never experience in her life, which had now been almost completely spent. She could hardly wait for the day to arrive.

It was a blustery, snowy day when it did come, and as he drove slowly down the unfamiliar street, looking for the house, he saw a woman standing outside in the cold, waiting. Their reunion after five decades was something too tender to describe. But he told me that when he was wishing her good-bye, he asked her, "Mom, is there anything I can do for you?" With tears running down her face she said, "Just love me, son. Just love me."

Why that plea? Because in her heart she had to have wondered how it was possible for him to love her when she had given him nothing. How could he love her without having any reason to love her? she must have thought. But to him, she had given the gift of life, and that was enough of a gift to cause Appreciative love to search for a way to express itself.

Was not that the reason for Kathy's search, too? Even though their meeting was brief, and her mother was hours away from death, for Kathy it brought healing—just to hear her mother say, "I love you." Kathy could have found love elsewhere. There was always that possibility. But even if she had, there would have been that longing etched in her heart—I wish I could find her. It was more than a search for love; it was the search for a particular love. This is more than a Need-love. It is the need of a particular love toward whom the heart is bent. It is born out of an Appreciative love for being.

The ultimate object and resource of that kind of love is God Himself, who has formed us, and the culminating response from us is more than just love. That response of appreciation, of gratitude, of awe, of surrender, of hunger to be consummated in the spirit is what we call worship. And until we have found Him who alone is worthy of worship, the heart searches in loneliness.

Just like the salmon that determinedly swims against rock and tide to return to where it was spawned and, having returned, gives birth to its own, so also does life spring from the one who has returned to his or her very source in worship, to God Himself.

There is a reason that both the conversation with the woman at the well and the interaction with the woman with the alabaster jar of ointment end on the theme of worship. Both women had loved and lost. Both knew the deception of love. Both had lived through Need-love and Gift-love. Both knew the limitations of pleasure. Now they came with an unparalleled Appreciative love. They bowed before their Savior and carried His message to all they knew.

THE RETURN TO OUR ROOTS

This takes us back, not to our behavior, but to our being from which we then instruct our behaving. Self-theorists can be pardoned, because their discipline can take them only to the so-called observable. They stop where secular presuppositions force them to stop. But they obviously fall short of the starting point, because we are not who we are because we do what we do. Rather, we do what we do because we are who we are. And the Scriptures remind us that we are fashioned by a loving God who calls us to worship Him.

I recently heard a most fascinating story of a young couple's journey to Romania. They went to adopt a little boy who was born without arms. As they visited him in the orphanage, they noticed that nobody would even look in little George's direction because his handicap was seen as an ill omen and a curse upon a family. But the young couple kept looking at this little boy and were determined to bring him back to the United States and raise him as their son if his mother would release him to them. But something unforgettable happened.

The mother, when contacted, looked at them and asked why

they wanted this child. "I have heard," she said, "that in America they use babies for genetic experimentation. Is that why you want to take my son?"

The would-be parents were as wise as they were selfless, and with the complete limitation of language, did something that could only have been inspired by God. They had brought a Romanian Bible with them, and they handed it to her, opened at Psalm 139. The Romanian woman took it in her hands and began to read:

> O LORD, you have searched me
> and you know me.
> You know when I sit and when I rise;
> you perceive my thoughts from afar.
> You discern my going out and my lying down;
> you are familiar with all my ways.
> Before a word is on my tongue
> you know it completely, O LORD.
>
> You hem me in—behind and before;
> you have laid your hand upon me.
> Such knowledge is too wonderful for me,
> too lofty for me to attain. . . .
>
> For you created my inmost being;
> you knit me together in my mother's womb.
> I praise you because I am fearfully and wonderfully made;
> your works are wonderful,
> I know that full well.
> My frame was not hidden from you
> when I was made in the secret place.
> When I was woven together in the depths of the earth,
> your eyes saw my unformed body.
> All the days ordained for me
> were written in your book
> before one of them came to be.

How precious to me are your thoughts, O God!
  How vast is the sum of them!
Were I to count them,
  they would outnumber the grains of sand. . . .

Search me, O God, and know my heart;
  test me and know my anxious thoughts.
See if there is any offensive way in me,
  and lead me in the way everlasting. (Ps. 139:1–6, 13–16, 23–24)

The mother wept through her reading of this passage and clutched the Bible to her heart. Then she gave her armless son into the arms of one who saw his outstretched being, not the absence of his outstretched arms.

Our beings long for God. He has fashioned our hungers. Only in Him is the soul hunger of loneliness met—not just in love but in worship. This mother knew that her little boy would grow up and want to see her. But she also knew that he would be pointed not just to the source of his life but to the source of her life, too. The clutching of the Scriptures was her expression of Appreciative love to God Himself.

Worship Is More Than Love

When worship is fully understood, it does at least three things that clearly counter the ache of loneliness.

The first recognition of worship is the legitimate sense of mystery and the rightful expression of awe. This thrilling recognition of mystery is one of the greatest fulfillments of the human heart. Take a good look at our pursuits in every avenue of knowledge. Why do the horizons of science continue to expand? Only because of our desire to know. And inevitably the more we uncover, the deeper we find the layers that remain. Our excavations reveal marvel after marvel, and we do not know what lies beneath it all. Some cynically quip that it is all DNA. Others go to the reductionistic end and pathetically say that it is all chemistry. Still others point to a primordial soup. But even the most informed secularistic thinkers admit that beyond a certain minuscule fragment of time the book of origins is silent.

Only recently, as the close-up surface of Mars was being viewed on our television screens, those who had worked on the project gave names to the rocks they saw and to the machines that they themselves made, and they stood in awe of matter because it is 120 million miles away. But it may not be thanked. How soon the first response of our wonder of exploration has died. Have we forgotten what the astronauts felt when they first went around the dark side of the moon and experienced "earthrise" over the horizon of the moon? The only suitable expression for them then was, "In the beginning God."

Now we are playing music to applaud the machines we have built. It is little wonder that we have learned to live with loneliness, because our mysteries have a very short shelf life. Is it possible that God who Himself is pure spirit has placed a particular kind of mystery within us so that only in awe of Him can we find perpetual novelty?

We are finite persons. When that finitude loses gratitude and is in awe of the impersonal, the branches of existence lose connection with the roots of essence, and behavior is studied detached from the mystery of life itself. Appreciation-pleasure becomes a poor and fleeting substitute for Appreciative love.

God warned Israel of old in His reiteration of the Law that the worst thing that could happen to them was to become an ungrateful people, thinking that by their own hands they had planted and reaped. He said to them in their infant stage as a nation: "I gave you a land on which you did not toil and cities you did not build; and you live in them and eat from vineyards and olive groves that you did not plant" (Josh. 24:13).

Repeatedly He reminded them, "I am the LORD your God that brought you out of the land of Egypt." If He drew attention to the fact that the land in which they lived was inherited and due to no merit of their own, if He reminded them that the very harvest they enjoyed was from vineyards they had not planted—how much more would He want us to remember that the very life we have is a gift? This reminder to ourselves again and again is at the heart of worship. If it were not for this kind of Appreciative love, one could never truly worship God. Out of a worship that is pure, all other loves gain their definition.

Second, not only does this kind of Appreciative love lead to worship that is alive with awe and wonder, it goes beyond itself and gives to others. This is also important to note, because the countering effect of worship in one's loneliness does not stop with the self; it then must reach out to others in their needs and struggles. If it were not for Appreciative love for God, one could never love his or her enemy or even love for another's sake.

Out of Appreciative love flows true Gift-love, given especially to those in the throes of Need-love. Because of our love for God we endure all things, and from the love with which He enriches us flows a love that is not our own. It comes from a deposit He makes in our hearts from which we draw.

In a world full of hate and suspicion, what a distinctive role the Christian can play. This is the only way in which the spread of alienation is arrested and the nearness of Christ's love is brought even nearer to so many who are lonely. All the hatred that is demonstrated in our world has resulted from a world that knows no Appreciative love toward the very author of life.

Finally, Appreciative love or worship not only flows out of gratitude to God and spreads the love of God in a hostile world, it also binds the worshiping life into a single focus, touching upon every sense of life itself. Many artists and gifted writers feel the ache of loneliness because theirs is a mangled genius. The "sword of Solomon" has done its work in their spirits, cutting them up. They are persons first before they are artists, and a life that seeks fulfillment in its expertise before it finds fulfillment in its being is bound to feel deeply the ache of fragmentation. Just as a child cannot be physically mangled and still retain wholeness, we cannot mangle ourselves essentially without the resultant sense of desolation. Worship brings the coalescence of essence.

CONCLUSION

Thomas Wolfe was right. The problem of loneliness is universal. The hymn-writer who penned the beloved Christmas carol "O Little Town of Bethlehem" captured this idea well in the words, "The hopes and fears of all the years are met in thee tonight."

D. H. Lawrence is right, too. Love is not the root; it is only the branches. When we turn to the author of love to define the source of its root and the reach of its branches, love is understood rightly and is elevated to the highest pinnacle but worships at a different altar. Each individual is a unique and distinctive offering brought to God in gratitude. To slightly alter Augustine—Our hearts are restless until they find their *worship* in Him.

The songwriter beautifully blends these truths, based on the forty-second Psalm:

> As the deer panteth for the water,
>   so my soul thirsteth after Thee,
> You alone are my heart's desire and I long to worship Thee.
> You alone are my strength and shield,
> To you alone may my spirit yield;
> You alone are my heart's desire, and I long to worship Thee.[10]

Seven

The Cry of God for His People

THE OPENING WORDS of any talk are of strategic value. Students of public speaking are challenged to learn the art of gaining an audience's attention. Often certain methods or ploys are resorted to for that very purpose. Then, having gained a hearing and communicated all that was intended, how that discourse is closed becomes of paramount importance. In one's closing thoughts, that which was meant to attract or was on the surface when it began is set aside for that which must remain and that which is at the core of the matter. In the closing, the listener must be left with the final implications and with the necessary imperatives, deduced from what has been said.

But this importance that we place on closing words is not only of value in a public setting. We all consciously or otherwise pay great heed to what we say in very private conversations or whenever we bid someone farewell. How we part, even for a few hours, or what we say when the absence will be extensive is carefully chosen. Our children often, with a teasing expression on their faces, preempt our words as they leave, because they know what is about to come forth—"We love you . . . be careful." In the southern United States, it is "Y'all come back, now." For the Spanish it is "adios," meaning "to God." The same is so in French—"adieu." In English "good-bye" is a contraction derived from "God be with you." We commit to a hope and a care and a prospect of meeting again each time we bid farewell.

When God gives us His opening and His closing words, there are no ploys, no gimmicks, only life-defining truth. We had better listen carefully, because if we are not going to be in His care and keeping when He bids farewell, there is no hope of faring well! The words of Jesus come to mind when He wept over His beloved city: "Look, your house is left to you desolate. For I tell you, you will not see me again until you say, 'Blessed is he who comes in the name of the Lord'" (Matt. 23:38–39). How important that "until" was. But for that caveat, the future would have been bleak.

The Scriptures open with the words "In the beginning, God." There is no other rational starting point for life than God. That is the axis upon which life turns. That is the source from which life begins. That is the reference from which all definitions arise.

What emerged immediately in the Genesis story was God's original intent to walk and to talk with His own creation. To commune with them. But then that communion was ruptured by Adam and Eve choosing their own terms of engagement.

When you notice Michelangelo's painting of God reaching out to Adam, you see how outstretched God's arm is. Every muscle on His face is contorted, and the hand is reaching as far as possible to make contact. By contrast, Adam lackadaisically lets a limpish hand dangle with apathy in an attitude that seems to say, "If it meets it meets." That reflects the contrasting inclinations of the heart very well.

As generations came and went, God sought out one in the midst of all creation, one who would understand His heart and be willing to be clasped in His hand. Abraham became that one man who was willing to do that and leave everything in search of a city whose builder and maker was God. He was paid the ultimate compliment by God, who called him "the friend of God."

But we notice two definitive lines that Abraham drew for his life. He was known as a man of the tent and as a man of the altar—life's transitoriness and life's sanctity. In short, the focal point of his whole being was an altar, and all of living was nothing more and nothing less than an extension of his worship. That was central to all that he did.

The succeeding generations made the same mistakes that the preceding ones had made. The tent and the altar gave way to a secularistic (which literally means this-worldly) pursuit, seeking the temporary and embracing the profane. The end result was a lost altar for the community and a bitter enslavement in Egypt. But God heard their cry and made a way for them to escape from that bondage. He led them out to a land of their own, one that was flowing with milk and honey. On that journey, after redeeming them and giving them the Moral Law, the very first thing God instructed them to do was to build a tabernacle, with particular attention to the altar. This makeshift structure was not a thing of permanence but a place of meeting that could be dismantled and taken with them as they journeyed.

About four centuries after their deliverance, as the so-called golden age of Israel was ushered in, one of the most ironic developments portended their collapse. David wished to build a temple. He was the sweet singer of Israel and a man after God's own heart. He longed for something grand that would envelope the nation's worship. He envisioned a more permanent structure rather than the skeletal and portable tabernacle. That story is told in 2 Samuel 7. Listen to God's rather blunt response to David:

> Are you the one to build me a house to dwell in? I have not dwelt in a house from the day I brought the Israelites up out of Egypt to this day. I have been moving from place to place with a tent as my dwelling. Wherever I have moved with all the Israelites, did I ever say to any of their rulers whom I commanded to shepherd my people Israel, "Why have you not built me a house of cedar?" (2 Sam. 7:5–7)

This significant change in Israel's history when the temple was erected became a turning point in the people's whole attitude toward

God. From being owned by God it was as if they now owned Him. From journeying *with* Him they now had to journey *to* Him. As God became immovably housed, spirituality became localized, and life became disconnected from worship. There came as a tragic result the glorification of a means that ultimately lost the ends.

I remember on one occasion being ushered in to speak at the Center for Geopolitical Strategy in Moscow. Some of Russia's biggest names either studied or taught there at some time. The general who accompanied me took me first to a large hall, ostentatiously appointed with royal colors, much inlaid with gold, and adorned with a wealth of art. The ceilings rose upward like that of a cathedral. Halfway to the ceiling, pictures of Russia's great generals surrounded the room, from Peter the Great to Kutuzov, of fame during the Napoleonic wars. There was no doubt that the entire building was meant to exalt Russia's heroes and, in effect, dwarf the common person as he or she entered.

How ironic, I thought, that a nation whose ideological cry was supposedly for the primacy of the worker had decorated its structures to a point where the worker felt insignificant. So subtle and contradictory are the results of our best intentions. Likewise, there was just cause in the elaborateness of the temple, but the postscript to the blueprint told a tale of wrecked intentions—both God and the people got lost.

Everything about the temple was luxurious, elegant, and spectacular. But everything that distorted worship began right there. It was there that the Book of the Law was lost. It was there that the sacrificial system became corrupted. It was there that the priests lost the nobility of their calling. It was there that the people lost God when His glory departed. The tent and the altar were replaced by a power-seeking ecclesiastical authority who in the midst of such ornateness deprived the people of their own priesthood.

God had desired to be tabernacled in each individual worshiper before they gathered for worship with one another. But the temple had taken over and now stood in the way. This was the entire thrust of Stephen's sermon in that historic seventh chapter of Acts. He paid for his boldness with his life. He said, "The Most High does not dwell in houses made with hands" (v. 48 RSV). It was a radical reminder that the people were not so much to go to the temple to worship but that they were to take their temples with them. Their bodies were to be the temple of God.

Let us be absolutely certain that this is not by any means to imply that the beauty and the structure of a place of worship have no importance. Hardly. It is only to suggest strongly that whenever a grand edifice is erected and huge images invade, literally or figuratively, the danger is always present of losing sight of the greater value of the ones who enter and of forgetting that the spires point upward, not to the earth. Everything in a place of worship speaks a language. Some speak silently, some intrusively. That is why the last words of God in the Old Testament, through the prophet Malachi, were a heartrending plea to the people to take a hard look at how worship had lost its worth. God's longing for His people had been thwarted, and a weariness had set in.

Interestingly enough, when John closed his Revelation, the last book of the New Testament, worship was his theme also. But he envisioned the culmination of authentic worship and, as stated earlier, said he saw no temple in the eternal city. God was not "house-bound" any longer.

A MODERN-DAY DILEMMA

We have looked at many themes as we have come this far: Guilt. Pleasure. Pain. God. Feelings. Loneliness. Now we come to understand how all of these are ultimately responded to in that commitment we call worship and why it is the consummate answer to the cries of the heart. In worship, our cries meet up with the cry of God's heart for His people—for that is what He seeks in us (see John 4:23). Without an understanding here, we will be disappointed in the Christian experience. The famed writer A. W. Tozer referred to worship as the missing jewel of the church.

When my family and I lived in England some years ago, a terrible windstorm hit much of the country. Thousands of trees were felled that night. Some days later we were walking outside Buckingham Palace, and my wife noticed something very significant. The trees themselves were huge and very tall, but their roots were unbelievably shallow. We stared at this disproportion and, not being horticulturally literate, we just talked about it and walked on.

We happened to be visiting some friends after that and expressed our surprise at the gigantic trees that were supported by such short roots. What we heard bore a fascinating lesson for life. The water level below the soil in England is so close to the surface that the roots do not have to penetrate very deep to find their nourishment. As a result, the roots stay shallow, and even though the trees are massive and sturdy on the outside, the first major storm uproots them with very little resistance offered.

What instruction is contained in that illustration. It is not sufficient to have roots; the roots must go deep. That is the goal we will now pursue. How do we build root systems capable of weathering every storm that seeks to draw us into the temporary and the profane?

We said earlier that love was not the root but was only the branches. The root, we indicated, was worship. But if our worship is shallow, the busyness of life and the distractions of our minds will fell the strongest of us no matter how sturdy we look outwardly.

Most of us will agree on this. As discomforting as it might be to us all, there is not a more pertinent theme that is needful in this hour for the church that God has called to Himself than this call to worship. For we too may have lost Him right there. So much corruption of worship is seen in our time that if one were to write out a biblical or systematic theology on the basis of what we observe in worship, God would be seen as one great mindless bundle of contradictions whose sole reason for existence is to bring some sort of physical bounce into our lives. Unless worship regains integrity, both in our personal lives and then in a community of believers, the cries of the heart will never find their rest, and God's outstretched hand will not meet ours.

A VOICE DECRYING THE WILDERNESS

Malachi's voice came at the end of the millennium that followed the Exodus. By the next time the nation would hear a prophetic voice, four hundred years would have elapsed. That is a long time in the history of a young nation. To live through twenty generations without a fresh voice calling to the people must have been terribly demoralizing to those who longed for righteousness to pour down like waters. But the voice of Malachi was really intended for them to stop and look back, far more than it was for them to look forward.

During those centuries, God had met them repeatedly, not only in one event after another, but in an obvious repetition of thought. From the days of the patriarchs all through the judges and the kings, the voice of God called His people to be a worshiping community. They had been called out from the run and ruck of human existence to value the altar and to understand what it meant to meet God.

You will recall how painstakingly God gave specifics for the design of the tabernacle. Every detail was given, including quantity and quality of material, measurements of the structure, the colors of the material, the naming of the artisans, and where the lines were to separate the rooms. Not only were the specifications given, but then they are repeated. Why all this importance? Why the absoluteness of the parameters? One can only infer that it was based on the purpose of the edifice—"There I will meet with you," God said (Exod. 29:42). "There I will commune with you." It is evidently of definitive value to God how we meet with Him and where.

The entire prophecy of Malachi has only fifty-five verses. That prophet's life message was summarized in a handful of words. But any brevity is offset by the potency and finality of his message. It was a time when nothing enormous threatened the historical landscape, so God was not seen as a person to be needed. The status quo offered no great fear.

It is said of the Book of Esther that it is the only book in the Bible where God is not mentioned, although He is inescapably present. It can be said of Malachi that God is abundantly present in reference (in fifty-three of the fifty-five verses there is a mention of God) yet conspicuously absent in the people's lives. If this book were taken to heart by each believer, it could be one of the most revolutionary changes ever to take place in our thinking, for these are the closing words of God over a particular period. Here the answer is given to every human cry in a most compelling way, for here, the cry of God's heart is given to us. What He seeks in us is true worship. For "the true worshipers . . . worship the Father in spirit and in truth, for they are the kind of worshipers the Father seeks. God is spirit, and his worshipers must worship in spirit and in truth" (John 4:23–24).

THE FIRST ELEMENT

Let us follow the train of thought in God's heart as the message opens. "'I have loved you,' says the LORD. But you ask, 'How have you loved us?'" This pattern of dialogue punctuates the book. "I say this, but you say 'How?'" "I make specific charges, and you deny them."

The mind-set is hard to fathom. One thousand years of history in which God had made certain assertions, and yet the people ask for clarification. Imagine the audacity of a chosen people to ask, "In what way have You loved us?"

I know of no better way to convey how unthinkable this response is than to share the stories of two prophets who illustrated God's love in the most graphic terms long before Malachi came on the scene. One of them spoke to the Northern Kingdom of Israel, the other to the Southern Kingdom of Judah. The way God spoke of His love through these two prophets is rather provocative. In fact, if we are to be completely forthright, the language and the metaphors are quite unsettling, if not sometimes embarrassing. But there is very good reason for it.

The first prophet is Hosea, who lived in the latter part of the eighth century before Christ. To him fell one of the most painful experiences of life. God commanded him to love a woman named Gomer who ultimately deserted him and then added shame to her betrayal by selling herself into prostitution. Out of this marriage came three children. The first was a son, who Hosea named Jezreel, meaning "judgment." The memory evoked in the Hebrew mind when the word *Jezreel* was used was of a day of reckoning, and a dreadful one at that.

Some time ago, my son and I visited the houses of Parliament in

London. Two painted masterpieces hang in one of the grand halls where foreign dignitaries are hosted for dinner. We were told that when French President Charles de Gaulle was hosted there for a banquet, he objected to being seated facing one of those paintings, which portrayed the battle of Waterloo. He asked to be moved so that his back was to that painting. The British complied. But much to his deeper anguish, he found himself now looking at the painting on the opposite wall, which was of another French defeat, the battle of Trafalgar.

No Frenchman would decorate his home with artistic reminders of those humiliating moments, let alone ever name his son "Waterloo" or "Trafalgar." There are Waterloos and Trafalgars in every nation's history, and the names and places associated with them become unpleasant reminders.

Yet in Hosea's house, the firstborn was called Jezreel, a warning that the specter of judgment hung over them, for it was at Jezreel that Jezebel met her pathetic and gruesome end. A famous sermon was once preached on that text, simply titled "Payday Someday."

Hosea's second child was a girl whom he named Lo-ruhamah, which meant "no more mercy." The nation had lived so long off the abundance of God's grace, which they had spurned, that God was now saying that "time has run out." There was no more mercy left for them. Even love can only go so far without prostituting itself in the process. Hosea's third child was a boy, and God said to call him Lo-Ammi, which meant "not my people." In strongly worded terms, God was saying "I disown you."

Imagine the mood in that home with three children named, in essence, Judgment, No More Mercy, and Not My People. Every time one of them was beckoned, there was a harsh reminder of spiritual adultery in the land. "Judgment, come to dinner." "No More Mercy, clean up your room." "Not My People, finish your homework."

But let us not overlook the one who bore the brunt of this betrayal. The worst pain in that home had to be the pain within Hosea's heart. For him the message was not just a sermon chastising the people and calling them back to God. He now knew better than anyone else what

God felt, because his was a thwarted love, too. His wife had left him and chose instead to live in the dreadful world of selling one's self to strangers for the love of money. Hosea surely stared at his motherless children and nursed his heart that was broken from an unrequited love. The struggle gave way to an inevitable question—"How long do I keep loving her?"

It was only a matter of time before the question moved outside the parsonage into the streets of the city where Hosea preached. A prophet of God who preached holiness was married to a woman who was a prostitute. "How can a holy man of God be joined to such an adulterous woman?" the people wondered and argued. One can only imagine the taunting Hosea got from those for whom it was all a mocking delight.

Picture this scene for a moment. A group of worshipers are walking to the place where they are to gather. They happen to pass by the brothel where the losers and the lost hang out, one of whom derisively shouts out to the throng headed to hear Hosea's message, "When you see him, tell him for me that some of us have bought his wife's services and have delighted in it. We are standing in line for more." Much shaken by this distasteful reality, somebody dares to broach the subject with Hosea and says, "Please tell us. How can a holy man like you be married to an adulterous woman like that?"

Hosea is silent for several moments and then says, "I have been waiting for you to ask. And I will be glad to tell you how easy it is to love a woman like that if you will first explain to me how a holy God can love an adulterous nation like us?"

If Hosea's silence before he answered was but for a few moments, the silence of the questioners must have seemed like an eternity. How could a people have missed that kind of love, which loved the unlovely, one that loved the undeserving, indeed, the disgusting?

Right from the beginning, God had reminded them that His love for them was not based upon the nation's size or strength or particular credit. It was completely an unmerited love, poured out without measure on a people who squandered it. God could have given that privileged status to Greece. But He did not. He could have given it to

Rome. But He did not. He could have given it to Babylon. But He did not. He looked at this tiny little nation, laughed at by Greece, bullied by Rome, enslaved by Babylon, and to it He said, "You alone have I loved of all the nations of the earth." His lovingkindness was shed upon them, though they were undeserving.

Billy Graham was once asked why God had chosen him to be the preacher to the world. He answered, "When I get to heaven, that will be my first question." We are all undeserving of His love, yet He loves us.

Several years ago there was an article in *The Christian Century* about a young drug addict in Harlem. It was written by a social worker who had this to say:

> He is dirty, ignorant, arrogant, dishonest, unemployable, broken, unreliable, ugly, rejected, alone. And he knows it. He knows at last that he has nothing to commend himself to another human being. He has nothing to offer. There is nothing about him which permits love of another person for him. He is unlovable. But it is exactly in his own confession that he does not deserve the love of another that he represents all the rest of us. For none of us is different from him in this regard. We are all unlovable. But more than that, the action of this boy's life points beyond itself to the Gospel. To God who loves us though we hate Him, who loves us though we do not satisfy His love, who loves us though we do not please Him. Who loves us freely, who accepts us though we have nothing to offer him. Hidden in the obnoxious existence of this boy is the scandalous secret of the Word Of God.[1]

There is a kind of scandalousness to such a love, isn't there? A love that loves the wantonly dissolute. A love that wills to love, though spurned. In Hosea, this is the point worth remembering: that God's rejected love, so flagrantly abused, was given the odious parallel of a woman who had left her husband to wallow and revel in a life of prostitution yet remained loved by him. That was the heart of Hosea's message in the late seven hundreds before Christ, principally to the Northern Kingdom.

Now let us move two hundred years later, and see what God had to say then. Once again, at the end of it we will ask why such crass metaphors. Through his prophet Ezekiel, on the eve of the fall of the Southern Kingdom of Judah, God gave an even more cutting description. In Ezekiel 16 He presented the following parable.

A man passed by the highways of this land one day. He saw a newborn baby, lying on the side of the road. He heard its cry and picked it up. He took it to the waters nearby, washed off all the afterbirth, wrapped the little one in soft pieces of cloth, and left her in compassionate care. Many years went by, and he passed through the land again. He saw a splendidly attractive young woman. He offered her his hand in marriage. She committed herself to him and to his love, and they were wedded.

Many years went by, and God said to the people, "I was the one who walked by and saw you in your destitution. I rescued you. I took you as a man would take his bride, and I loved you. Now after years of being married to you, you have forsaken my love."

And then He said this: "Every prostitute receives a fee, but you give gifts to all your lovers, bribing them to come to you from everywhere for your illicit favors. So in your prostitution you are the opposite of others; no one runs after you for favors. . . . For you give payment and none is given to you" (Ezek. 16:33–34).

God is in effect saying that Israel was worse than those who sold themselves for money. At least a prostitute has this in her defense—she is paid by her lovers to lie with her. "You are worse," He said. "You have paid your lovers to lie with you."

There is no more graphic picture of degeneration than this. At one stage harlotry was the lowest point. Then their hearts found something even lower. The seduction was no longer for the self-exonerating purpose of monetary gain but sheer brute-fashioned indulgence. Wrong for wrong's sake. A shameless, reckless, promiscuous life. Could one sink any lower than that? Yes. To our utter disbelief there was one more stage. From Hosea to Ezekiel we move to Malachi.

When another two hundred years elapsed, God said to them, "I have loved you."

They responded by saying, "How have You loved us?"

Had they forgotten what Hosea had said? Had they forgotten what Ezekiel had said? Of all the forces in the world, love is the most potent and the most vulnerable. When love has spent itself and has gone unrecognized, what is there left to do or to say except to take the heartbreak and the rejection? The people had sunk so low that they had lost the capacity to recognize love even as they were in the embrace of its abuse.

One recalls the words of the prophet Isaiah, through whom God said to His people, "What more could I have done for you that I have not already done?" If God could say that centuries before the cross, we can only wonder what He would want to ask this modern world that has rejected Him even after the cross. What does one say to a heart that does not recognize love in its supreme sacrifice?

Some years ago I was visiting one of Mother Teresa's homes, called Nirmal Hriday, in Calcutta, India. It literally means "pure heart." The sign outside the door instructed ambulance drivers to bring in only the destitute, those who had even been turned away by the hospitals because they were too close to death to be helped.

As I walked through this home, I saw one man who was probably fairly young but looked as if he were dying from old age. Emaciated and wearing a completely tired expression on his face, he was being held in the arms of a European woman who was feeding him with a dropper. I turned to my wife and said, "This is possibly the first time since he was a baby that someone has held him close." His eyes, as he stared up at the nurse, bespoke volumes of gratitude.

Is it not a thing to ponder that across cultures, beliefs, ethnicity, and language, love bears such a recognizable face that we affirm its beauty? Yet God had spent a thousand years demonstrating His love for His people, and with calloused hearts they cried out almost with one voice, "How have You loved us?"

I must confess that when I first began my study of the Old Testament in my graduate school days, I often pondered why such severe yet tender, crass albeit weighty, analogies were needed to express what had gone on between God and His people. Why such dramatic portrayals as those of Hosea and Ezekiel? What was the point of them all? Was there not a more sophisticated and genteel, less melodramatic way of saying the same thing? Was God resorting to extremes and provoking shock in the reader?

This raw expression of love was carried all the way to the cross. It was a profound awakening within me when I realized that God wants us to understand not just the doctrinal fact of His love but also the emotional intensity and the reality of His love. Love is not only a word describing commitment, as vital as that is. It is also a concept that engenders feeling.

In volumes of words, thinkers and theologians have debated and discussed the nature of God's feelings and whether or not He has them. We are all much indebted for all the effort and thought that has been spent on this theme and for the extent to which the subject has been tackled. But after all is read and studied, I find it inescapable that whatever tact some schools of thought have used to escape God's capacity to feel, I sincerely doubt God would have chosen the imagery that He has if it were not for His heart that comes through in such an utterance, "I have loved you."

There may be something that could help us here. We know that animals feel pain and even happiness. But we are equally cognizant that we would not credit them with the same capacity to comprehend pain or happiness as humans do in the very same situations. In fact, even within the animal world we know of different levels at which they express emotions. C. S. Lewis talked about the way we "spell pain." Pain, for example, for human beings is inevitably connected to a moral context and to questions of purpose, justice, and causality. We try to deal with it in terms of good and evil. There is a moral context within which we live, and hence there is a superiority in our moral reasoning when compared to the animal world. Why do we not think it possible for God to feel in a higher manner, within His own infinitude, but to nevertheless feel? He may "spell" joy and pain differently, in a way that transcends our capacity, without diminishing Himself or the reality of our understanding.

Thomas Aquinas reminded us of the analogical use of language; by analogy God can use the same word to describe His feelings and do so in a meaningful way while at the same time exceed our context. For example, when I say I love somebody and that person refuses to love me, I hurt. I hurt because I have lost something. When God says He loves us and we refuse to love Him, He hurts, too. But He hurts because *we* have lost something, not because *He* has lost something. The word is identical, but the context has a bearing on the use of the word.

This was the double tragedy of Israel. God said to them, "I love you," yet in their failure to recognize that love, they had also failed to see what they had lost. They did not, in the process of rejecting God's love, make God less than God. They made themselves less than they were meant to be.

In God's boldly stated love where He uses such emotionally laden terms, we understand the first component of meaningful worship: *One cannot worship without love,* which means the emotions are an intrinsic part of worship. But let us be absolutely sure that emotions and emotionalism are not the same thing. When emotions hijack the intellect, then a destructive element has entered in. The emotions harnessed and informed by truth make for a legitimate expression. Love is a vital part of worship.

WHERE IS THE HONOR?

God continued to speak through Malachi. He made a second charge: "A son honors his father, and a servant his master. If I am a father, where is the honor due me? If I am a master, where is the respect due me?" says the LORD Almighty. ". . . But you ask, 'How have we shown contempt for your name?'" (Mal. 1:6).

This was God's plea to them. He had tried in all of His efforts to get close to them. Having come close, they not only lost sight of His love, they also lost that all-important attitude of reverence. What a costly blunder, to have the Lord of glory come near and to forget who He is! This was shortsightedness of the worst kind.

In the Hindi language, the word for father is *Pita.* (The i has a soft sound, as in "it.") The word for mother is *Mata.* (The a has the same sound as in "father.") The important thing to know is that you do not call your father *Pita* or your mother *Mata,* even though those are the correct words. You always add the suffix *jee.* You call your father Pita-*jee* and your mother Mata-*jee,* because *jee* denotes respect and reverence. The closest parallel in the West would be in the southern United States, where children answer their father, "Yes, *sir,*" and their mother, "Yes, *ma'am*" while also calling them "Daddy" and "Mommy," a child's terms of endearment. So that which is dearest is also revered, maintaining a distance. In contemporary application, what God is really saying to His people is, "You call me *Daddy,* where is the *Sir?*"

When I was a little boy sometime in the 1950s, the renowned American athlete Jesse Owens paid a visit to India. I was thrilled to be in the front row observing his every move as he spoke of his triumphs in the 1936 Olympics in Berlin, where he ran under Hitler's glare and intimidation and won four gold medals. One can imagine the thrill of a youngster to be so close to a "hero." He described every event in which he competed and talked of the pressure and yet, the triumph of it all. After his talk, as the crowd surrounded him for autographs, I managed to get even closer, right next to his side. I just leaned toward him, making sure that at all times some part of me was in contact with some part of him.

Perhaps feeling my body pressed against his, he turned, bent down, reached out, and shook my hand. I lost sight of it in his big hand. He asked me for my name; I was so nervous, I am not even sure I got that right. But that handshake was to leave me staring at my hand on repeated occasions. *This was the hand that Jesse Owens shook.* All of my friends for years wished that either Jesse Owens or I had never been born. For no matter what the conversation, somehow I would find a reason to say, "When I was with Jesse Owens . . ."

Suppose for a moment that once Jesse Owens had shaken my hand I had lost the distinction between his greatness in athletics and my contrasting inability. Would that not have been the height of folly?

Now that he had come close was there sufficient reason for me to have patted him on the back and said, "All right, Jesse. It's just you and me—one on one. To the track we go"?

He was still the champion of the world, and I was just an admirer. Getting close did not bridge that difference. He was not Jesse to me just because we had shaken hands. He was still Jesse Owens, Sir.

This is the point that God is raising with His question. "Why do you have no reverence for Me?" "Have you lost sight of who I am?" This interaction between God and His people is a strong reminder of the second component of worship: *We cannot worship Him without reverence.*

When the high priest used to enter the Holy of Holies, which He did once a year, he had to enter backward, for he could not come "face to face" with God. When Uzzah, well-intentioned, reached out to steady the Ark of the Covenant, God gave the people a dramatic reminder that He was not to be handled as if He were a common thing. His presence was represented in the Ark of the Covenant.

This concept of honor and reverence is an extremely difficult one, especially in North America, where social distinctions are removed. The breakdown of social barriers is a good thing, but there are some distinctions that ought never to be erased to the extent that legitimate respect is lost, such as with parent/child, teacher/student, and youth/old age. When these distinctions are lost, something of life's direction has been lost for all of us. The greatest difference, of course, is between God and us, His creation. When that distinction is lost along with reverence, the greatest of all relationships dies.

It is interesting to note that just as reverence has died in our culture, the language has changed, too. We no longer have levels of addressing those who are our seniors or even those under whom we work or serve. Here too there were reasons for the changes, and important ones at that. But the end result is that the "You" when we talk to God and the "you" when we talk to our fellow human beings has lost its necessary distinction.

In the tenth chapter of Acts we read how Cornelius fell at the feet of Peter, and Peter lifted him up, saying, "Stand up, I am only a man"

(v. 26). The implication is clear. To fall on our knees before God is a legitimate expression and came naturally even for one who was, in the terms of that day, a pagan. Not only is praise due to God—which we hear so much about—but so is honor, about which we hear so little. In that beautiful King James translation of Psalm 111:9, we read "Holy and reverend is his name." The New International Version reads "Holy and awesome is his name." Today "awesome" is used to describe anything from basketball players to computers, and hence with that corruption, *reverence* may well be the better word for God.

In the letter to the Hebrews, even as the writer draws to his powerfully worded conclusion hailing Jesus as the "great high priest," the supreme revelation of God the Father, and the better way over all the angels, he charges us all, "Therefore, since we are receiving a kingdom that cannot be shaken, let us be thankful, and so worship God acceptably with reverence and awe, for our 'God is a consuming fire'" (Heb. 12:28).

Love and reverence are the first two components of integrity in worship.

SACRIFICING THE SICK

There is a third component to worship that God introduced, and He did so in His response to their belligerent question, "How have we shown contempt for your name?" (Mal. 1:6).

He answered, "'By saying that the LORD's table is contemptible. When you bring blind animals for sacrifice, is that not wrong? When you sacrifice crippled or diseased animals, is that not wrong? Try offering them to your governor! Would he be pleased with you? Would he accept you?' says the LORD Almighty" (1:7–8).

In this interaction we get to the heart of their predicament: *It is impossible to worship without sacrifice,* the giving of our best. But the people had begun to show contempt for God by bringing the lame and the blind and the sick of their fold and giving their leftovers to God as their worship.

When I was about twelve or thirteen years old, I was asked by our Sunday school teacher if I would be willing to play Joseph in the nativity mime that Christmas. I must add as kindly but as truthfully as I can that the church itself was so rankly liberal that the gospel was lost under the weight of ceremony. I was on the verge of saying no to this request, for I really did not know what all that meant. But then I was told what I would need to do: basically, to walk Mary to the altar with her arm in mine, stand there, turn around, have her put her arm in mine again, and walk out. No words, no big acting skill needed. When I met who was going to play Mary, I decided this would be quite a thrill.

I arrived at the church early and was walking around with time to kill. On a table at the altar, I saw a silver bowl with wafers in it. Having very little knowledge of what this could be, I took a handful of those wafers and enjoyed them as I admired all the great art and statuary in that fine cathedral. Suddenly I saw the vicar coming out of the vestry and walking straight toward me. I politely greeted him and continued my enjoyment of the biscuits in hand. He stopped, stared, and quite out of control, shouted, "What are you doing?"

As surprised by his outburst as he was at my activity, I said, "I am Joseph in the nativity mime."

That evidently was not what he was asking. "What is that in your hand?" he demanded. As he stared me down from head to toe, he could see that there was more in my pocket, too. I received the most incomprehensible tongue-lashing to which I had ever been subjected. The word that the priest kept repeating was the word *sacrilege.* I chose never to check out its meaning, for I was sure this was the end of the line for me, having done something I did not even know how to pronounce.

Years later, I could not help but chuckle when I was reading G. Campbell Morgan's definition of *sacrilege.* He said that it is normally defined as taking something that belongs to God and using it profanely. We all know the instance in the Book of Daniel when Belshaazar took the vessels in the temple and used them for his night of carousing and blasphemy. That was a sacrilegious use. But sacrilege, said Morgan, does not only consist of such profane use. In its worst form it consists of taking something and giving it to God when it means absolutely nothing to you. That was the charge God brought against His people when He said, "You bring the lame and the blind and the sick as an offering, is that not wrong?"

Worship at its core is a giving to God of all that is your best. This cannot be done without the sacrifice of the acclaim and adulation of the world. If we were to only pause for a few moments and take stock, we would see how close we all come to sacrilege each day.

Do we give Him the best of our time?

Do we give Him the best of our energies?

Do we give Him the best of our thinking?

Do we give Him the best of our wealth?

Do we give Him the best of our dreams and plans?

Or does the world get our best while God merely gets the leftovers? Charles Wesley wrote a beautiful hymn:

O Thou who camest from above
The pure celestial fire to impart.
Kindle a flame of sacred love
On the mean altar of my heart!

There let it for Thy glory burn
With inextinguishable blaze,
And trembling to its source return
In humble prayer and fervent praise.

Jesus, confirm my heart's desire
To work and speak and think for Thee;
Still let me guard the holy fire,
And still stir up Thy gift in me.

Ready for all thy perfect will,
My acts of faith and love repeat,
Till death Thine endless mercies seal,
And make the sacrifice complete.[2]

"To *work* and *speak* and *think* for thee." I think of those words often. How sad it is to live in a society with a prevalent mind-set that the smart ones in this world are deemed to be those in "secular professions" of numerous intellectual demands and hence, they are due respect. There is a not-so-subtle assumption these days that those in ministry are somehow not on a par intellectually, that God gets the remnants of the world's minds.

There is an ironic sense in which this is true. God has taken the weak of this world to confound the wise and the simple to counter the sophisticated. But there is a faulty sense in which this is then caricatured to imply that the thinking and the capable are of no interest to God or that the keenest thinkers belong to the world and the mediocre thinkers to God. Two of the finest minds in the Old and the New Testaments were Moses and Paul. They were called upon to bring those abilities into God's service, even as Abraham and Job in their wealth, were called upon to recognize their spiritual poverty at the altar of God.

Four years before he paid for his commitment to God with His life, William McChesney, who was martyred in 1964 when he was a missionary in the Congo, wrote from his home in Phoenix, Arizona:

> If he be God, and died for me,
> No sacrifice too great can be
> For me, a mortal man, to make—
> I'll do it all for Jesus' sake.[3]

THE CORRUPTION OF INTENT

We have seen that one cannot worship without emotion, one cannot worship without reverence, and one cannot worship without sacrifice. Now we come to the fourth component, which is that *it is impossible to worship God with a wrong motive.* God cries out, "'Oh, that one of you would shut the temple doors, so that you would not light useless fires on my altar! I am not pleased with you,' says the LORD Almighty, 'and I will accept no offering from your hands'" (Mal. 1:10).

So much in the temple had become a show. Everything seemed to point to how impressive one's religious performance and duties appeared. But deep inside, the heart was far, far away from God. Anytime we find a blend of power and ceremony with the need for inward purity, there is a great risk that the latter will suffer. The monotony of repetition and the seduction of power are two extremely potent forces to contend with. That is what makes the whole concept of staying fresh in one's study and efforts so necessary. Every new day places a new opportunity before us to be refreshed and to learn, to reinforce and to renew. "Oh! that someone would shut the door," God pleads. Enough of this charade.

At least figuratively speaking, the heart is the seat of the soul. We mean by that that our inclinations, our passions, our desires, our sincerity are true intimations in matters of the spirit. It is our wordless expression of true commitment. The old song said it in physical terms, "Your lips are so near, but where is your heart?" That is precisely what God is asking in spiritual expression. Their comings and goings in the temple were very obvious, but their hearts were far away.

A DEARTH OF INSTRUCTION

Next God brought to the people the fifth component in worship: that *it is impossible to worship God without instruction in the truth.* He calls upon the priests and takes them to task. "For the lips of a priest ought to preserve knowledge, and from his mouth men should seek instruction—because he is the messenger of the LORD Almighty" (Mal. 2:7).

Is there a clearer mandate or a more sobering trust than this—to instruct people in the knowledge of God so that they might worship Him not only in spirit but also in truth? Worship can be erroneous in form, and we may all at times make those errors in form. But the great danger before us is not the errors in form as much as it is in the corruption of substance. Observe the next time when the emotions run wild, and pause to ask the all-important question: Is this merely a distortion in ceremony, or is this plundering the very nature of God?

So often immodesty and disorder have taken over, and expression has been given license. How unsettling and confusing this trend has become to Christendom at large, to say nothing of the skeptic. In the days when God gave priestly instructions, He warned that if there was even a callus on his hand the priest should refrain from his duties till the callus was gone, for no distraction ought to interfere with the concentration of the worshiper. How far have we strayed from such injunctions. Worship is not for the glory of men and women; it is for the glory of God.

Teaching is the seed sown within the heart and mind from which the fruit is produced in life that can then be brought as a sacrifice to God. Where there is no teaching, the harvest can become blighted, if not useless.

THE HOME—THE HEART OF THE CHURCH

This brings us to the final component that God placed before His people, the charge of broken promises or of wanton disobedience, for *it is impossible to worship God without obedience.* Here the specific point that God was making is utterly surprising. He went back into their homes and asked them to take honest note of the broken promises that husbands had made to their wives and that wives had made to their husbands. He brought the tragedy of a nation that had lost its relationship with God right down to the marital vows. How important this must have been for Him to incorporate it into His closing words.

> Another thing you do: You flood the LORD's altar with tears. You weep and wail because he no longer pays attention to your offerings or accepts them with pleasure from your hands. You ask, "Why?" It is because the LORD is acting as the witness between you and the wife of your youth, because you have broken faith with her, though she is your partner, the wife of your marriage covenant.
>
> Has not the LORD made them one? In flesh and spirit they are

> his. And why one? Because he was seeking godly offspring. So guard yourself in your spirit, and do not break faith with the wife of your youth. (Mal. 2:13–15)

In the old English usage, the marriage vow was made: "With my body I thee worship." This pledged an unqualified exclusiveness in consummating love. God said, "You have broken those vows and betrayed the wife of your youth." In other words, worship had collapsed through a disobedient lifestyle that fed into the sanctity of the home and that, in turn, returned as a hypocritical worship. Of all the unexpected themes one could have encountered in Malachi when God was talking about worship, this theme of keeping one's marital vows would have been the least expected. Yet this is precisely what God has dealt with at length.

Worship in disarray leads all the way back to the home in broken covenants. If the word that we have committed to God Himself is not honored, what motivation is there to honor our word to our husbands or wives? The domino effect then sets in, and ungodly offspring are raised when vows are broken. God said that it grieved Him much to see the loss of the children trapped in a situation with broken commitments. This is a sobering thought that's painful to reflect upon.

Think for a moment of that startling verse in the Book of James (5:12) when he defined true religion. Think of the numerous possibilities such a statement could have elicited. Yet, he defined true religion very simply as, "Let your 'Yes' be yes, and your 'No,' no." In other words, honor your word. The people had become content to live out a lie, and mutual destruction had set in. A dishonorable family life converged in the worship of the community, and a dishonorable life of worship had made its way into the home.

The problem could therefore be stated even in a reverse form: If the temple was filled with those who could not be trusted in their marital commitments, how could they be trusted in their commitment to God? In the eyes of God, who we are in private does matter; it determines what we have a right to say or to do in public. Modern-day political theory has taken power and ceremony and severed it from character. That which God has joined together, let no one put asunder. The same is true in worship.

"How can you come to the temple," He asked, "when the temple of your body has been profaned?" "Who may ascend the hill of the LORD . . . [but] he who has clean hands and a pure heart?" (see Ps. 24:3). God brought the rupture of worship right down to where it mattered the most—in this earthly tabernacle where He wants to meet with us and where He wants to dwell with us. We cannot worship Him without moral purity.

God's purpose for us has always been in that sequence: redemption, righteousness, worship. We cannot be righteous until we are first redeemed. We cannot worship until we are redeemed and righteous. He followed that same sequence in Israel's history. First He redeemed them. Then He gave them the Law to point them to righteousness. Finally, He gave them the instructions for worship. The peril of a life that is not living for His honor, finding in its place a substitute in worship, is a violation of the nature of God.

A COLLAPSED WORSHIP EQUALS A WEARY LIFE

Can we see now what had happened in the collapse of Israel's worship? The corruption was systemic, and that was the reason God described the resultant condition when He said, "'And you say, "What a burden!" and you sniff at it contemptuously,' says the LORD Almighty" (Mal. 1:13). "You have said, 'It is futile to serve God'" (Mal. 3:14), or, as the King James Version translates it, "What a weariness is it!" (Mal. 1:13). For anyone who is determined to live in dishonesty, worship will be a burden.

Anytime worship has lost its worth a weariness will set in, and a sense of the futility of life will take over. Unwittingly or otherwise, even the ordinary, unstudied person can see the connection between futility or barrenness and the loss of worship.

A barrenness of spiritual life brings its own judgment—more barrenness. When vain repetitions become a habit, we repeat all the more, and further futility becomes the result. This may be the reason for the way worship in our time has degenerated into more ignorance as novelty gives way to more novelty.[4]

In 1976, *Reader's Digest* printed a little satire entitled, "The Noah Way," which illustrates this kind of spiritual barrenness:

> And the Lord said unto Noah, "Where is the ark which I have commanded thee to build?"
>
> And Noah said unto the Lord, "Verily, I have had three carpenters off ill. The gopher-wood supplier hath let me down—yea, even though the gopher-wood hath been on order for nigh upon 12 months. What can I do, O Lord?"
>
> And God said unto Noah, "I want that ark finished even after seven days and seven nights."
>
> And Noah said, "It will be so."
>
> And it was not so. And the Lord said unto Noah, "What seemeth to be the trouble this time?"
>
> And Noah said unto the Lord, "Mine subcontractor hath gone bankrupt. The pitch which thou commandest me to put on the outside and on the inside of the ark hath not arrived. The plumber hath gone on strike. Shem, my son who helpeth me on the ark side of the business, hath formed a pop group with his brothers, Ham and Japheth. Lord, I am undone."
>
> And the Lord grew angry and said, "And what about the animals, the male and the female of every sort to come to thee to keep their seed alive upon the face of the earth?"
>
> And Noah said, "They have been delivered unto the wrong address, but should arriveth on Friday."
>
> And the Lord said, "How about the unicorns and the fowls of the air by sevens?"
>
> And Noah wrung his hands and wept, saying, "Lord, unicorns are a discontinued line; thou canst not get them for love nor money. And fowls of the air are sold only in half dozens. Lord, Lord, thou knowest how it is."

> And the Lord in His wisdom said, "Noah, my son, I knowest. Why else do you think I have caused a flood to descend upon the earth?"

This could well have been written for today. We, too, like Israel of old, have followed the gradual mangling of the individual and the community, from the loss of love and gratitude to God, all the way to a weak-willed, disobedient lifestyle. For us, too, there is a weariness within and without. People then sought, each in his or her own pursuit, some way of assuaging their hunger. For some, guilt became unbearable. For others, feelings outran knowledge, and worship lost its truth. Many lost their concept of who God was. Most experimented with pleasures that left them empty. The righteous could not understand how pain served any purpose. The home became a place of broken vows, rupturing families and wounding children. And for all a deep-seated loneliness pervaded their lives.

Somewhere in the midst of their ceremony and ritual, a weariness had come in, and the purpose of God communing with them was lost. That is why His last plea before the very Son of God appeared as God "tabernacled" (dwelled) with them was for them to understand what worship was meant to be and to do.

Archbishop William Temple has left us with what I consider the most beautiful definition of that intent:

> Worship is the submission of all of our nature to God. It is the quickening of conscience by His holiness, nourishment of mind by His truth, purifying of imagination by His beauty, opening of the heart to His love, and submission of will to His purpose. All this gathered up in adoration is the greatest of all expressions of which we are capable.[5]

In short, worship is what binds all of life together and gives it a single focus. Conscience. Mind. Imagination. Heart. Will. All knit together in worship, for here love, reverence, sacrifice, motive, truth, and obedience are harnessed before the one who made us, who alone can bring unity in the diversity with which He has fashioned us. The breakdown in most of our thinking occurs when we allow ourselves to become fragmented and life loses its focus. Worship takes the diversity of our loves and abilities and coalesces them into a direction in life.

Now we can see how worship responds to guilt, for with reverence we come to Him for forgiveness.

Now we can see why worship goes beyond the satisfaction of pleasure, for even pleasure has its weariness.

Now we can see how worship guides our feelings, for even our feelings need to be bound and informed by truth.

Now we can see how worship needs to know who God is, for we come to Him on His terms, as Daddy-Sir, or Holy Father.

Now we can understand how worship counters the sense of loneliness, because loneliness cannot be dispelled by love alone. Only worship can bind all our passions, something love cannot do.

This is the reason that worship is the supreme expression in life, the root from which life's branches grow and expressions flower. The words of Eric Liddell in the film *Chariots of Fire* are very significant. Before he went as a missionary to China, he ran in the 1924 Olympics and won the gold medal in his event. When he was asked why he spent so much time practicing, he said: "God has made me for a purpose, for China. But He has also made me fast, and when I run I feel His pleasure."

Worship is coextensive with life. Here the sacred and the secular meet. Here our cries meet the cry of God.

Postscript to Chapter 3

The Cry for a Reason in Suffering

CONFIDENCE IN God's character is at the heart of the philosophical struggle that ensues when one is confronted by the question of evil. The skeptic's question has to be answered: Would you create a world with such pain, and if you did, could you at the same time still be called good? This is not an easy challenge, because a great deal of assumption and deduction flow into the question and out from the answer.

Keeping the response at its most foundational level, one may draw at least two inferences when the question of evil and the existence of God is raised. The first is the obvious one: How can there be an all-loving and all-powerful God when evil is so evident and uncontained? The second is a little more unsettling. Even if God exists, how can He be called good while allowing death and destruction to happen, when we ourselves would be considered wicked if we did the same thing?

That was the question of Ivan Karamazov: Would *you* structure a universe that allowed such heinous tragedies? How can God allow all that we see and hear and still be called good? This question has to be first viewed in its broader implications before its more forthright and blunt challenge can be addressed.

We are all familiar with the general way in which the question is often phrased. C. S. Lewis has penned it in the following terms:

> If God were good, He would wish to make His creatures happy, and if God were almighty He would be able to do what He wished. But the creatures are not happy. Therefore God either lacks goodness, or power, or both. This is the problem of pain, in its simplest form. The possibility of answering it depends on showing that the terms good and almighty and perhaps also the term happy are equivocal: for it must be admitted from the outset that if the popular meanings attached to these words are the best, or the only possible, meanings, then the argument is unanswerable.[1]

For our purposes, the question has to be taken further. What the skeptic has really said is that if we did what we see God doing or if we allowed what God allows, we would be considered wicked. So how is it good when God makes such decisions but evil if we were to do the same?

THE PHILOSOPHICAL DIMENSION

Before any specific answer to this question can be given, let us first restate an important point that was made in Chapter 3, "The Cry for a Reason in Suffering," where we looked at Job's struggle with God and with evil. This all-important point must undergird the answer: that the existence of God cannot be disproved by introducing the reality of evil or wickedness. Those categories only exist if an absolute moral law exists. And an absolute moral law exists only if God exists.

Now, one might try to skirt the issue and say, "But we do not see a moral law in existence; therefore, there cannot be a moral lawgiver." But that only removes the issue one step further by implying that a moral law would be recognizable to us if we saw it. The assumption here is that we have the capacity to decide whether or not a moral law exists. How have we acquired that capacity in a purely naturalistic universe? The truth is that no matter how much we may try, we cannot deny a moral frame of reference without invoking a moral absolute. To put it simply, if we grant the currency of evil in this world, God is not expendable.

THE MORAL DIMENSION

Now let us go on to the question of how God can be sovereign over a world in which some of the realities that exist would be deemed unquestionably evil if they were authorized by us. To fully answer that question we must make a step-by-step approach.

First, we must make the connection between God's character and His relation to the moral law. Is the moral law a moral law just because God has decreed it such and therefore it is arbitrary, or is the moral law ultimate, superintending even over Him? In other words, is the moral law something whimsically uttered by God or something abstract that exists apart from Him? Does He operate by raw power and make choices that are then deemed good only because He says they are so, or is He Himself under the law, having to obey it even against His own wishes?

My response to these questions begins with a counterquestion: Is the moral law by which each one of us chooses to live a law that we have arbitrarily chosen by which to exercise our power, or does it exist over and above us? If we have arbitrarily chosen it, then we have no right to condemn the moral law by which anyone else operates, including God. On the other hand, if the moral law stands over and above us, then how do we determine where it comes from? This question stumps the atheist and every other world-view, be it pantheistic or even in some instances, theistic.

For the Christian, the answer as implicitly given in the Old and the New Testaments is that the moral law that calls for the sanctity of every individual life is given to us by God, and this is why we think inescapably in a moral frame of reference. We cannot shake it off. For centuries every argument Christian philosophers have used to defend the existence of God has been attacked or countered, but the moral struggle with which we all live makes the moral argument inescapable. Thus the question resurfaces. If the moral law haunts us and the moral law comes from God, is it decreed by Him or is He also subject to it? Once again, is it arbitrary or ultimate?

As we begin to unfold the answer to this question, a vital point of distinction must be made between us, as finite creatures, and God, an infinite being. We need very clearly to understand that the two choices of whether the law is arbitrary or ultimate only exist for us as finite beings because our finitude cannot allow for other possibilities and our character cannot be the source of absolutes. Man cannot be the measure of all things, or else we would be forced to ask, Which man will be the ultimate measure?

In the name of religion and in the name of atheistic ideologies, millions have been killed. We must put away our illusion that "man is basically good." History and experience tell us in blood and tears that we cannot trust our character. But with God, the law is neither arbitrary nor over Him; it is rooted *in* His character, which is perfect and unchanging. He alone eternally and perfectly exists. Just as the reason for His existence is in Himself, so too is the moral law. The reason for *our* existence is outside of ourselves, as is the moral law.

There is no falsehood in God. There is no evil bent or false judgment in God. God never makes a misjudgment. He never acts for purposes that are ill-willed or destructive of that which is good. Only that which is pure and righteous is intrinsic to God Himself. That is why no so-called tragedy or atrocity ought to be interpreted in the vacuum of the two choices of arbitrary or ultimate but from within the character of the one who is all powerful and all good.

What does this actually mean in the twists and turns, in the hurts and losses, of our earthly existence? Let us apply that frame of reference.

THE EXISTENTIAL REALITY

When a tragedy or atrocity strikes, there are at least four distinct "victims" in that act or event. One is the person whose life may have been lost in that happening. (Let us suppose it is a child, since that is the way the skeptic always tosses that question at a Christian.)

We must immediately pause and analyze the heart and mind of the question. In the purview of God, is such an act, one that results in the loss of a child's life, really an act without recovery? God is the author of life and has the power to restore it to the one who has "lost" it. *We* may perceive that life to be lost, but to the giver of life it is not lost. And to one who knows Him the recovery is even greater than the life lived in the flesh. That is why the apostle says, "For to me, to live is Christ and to die is gain" (Phil. 1:21).

How can dying be gain unless it is to a life more beautiful and ultimate than the life that is now "dead"? In the death of a child, the Scriptures give us every indication that the child goes to be with God. Not, I might add, because of a moral perfection in the child but because of the provision of the cross. When he lost his son, David said, "I will go to him, but he will not return to me" (2 Sam. 12:23). There was a finality to the earthly existence but not to existence itself. The life that is "lost" is not lost when it is in the hands of the one who made it and sustains it.

The second one who suffers is the one who, though he or she knows Christ's redeeming grace, bears the bereavement and must survive the loss of that loved one. The view from the hearse is a painful one. But here, God is the comforter and the healer who brings the consolation of His presence to the one who carries that pain. Read some of the magnificent psalms of consolation written by David when he bore his grief and loss. In the most famous of all his psalms, David declared, "Even though I walk through the valley of the shadow of death, I will fear no evil, for you are with me; . . . and . . . [you] comfort me" (Ps. 23:4).

Across history the greatest testimonies of the all-encompassing grace of God have been demonstrated, not as psychological ploys, but because of the real presence of God in the life of one who lives with that pain. God not only gives inner healing and sustenance but the promise that those who have been separated will meet again.

Relationships that are made in God never die. The apostle Paul said, "Ye sorrow not, even as others which have no hope" (1 Thess. 4:13 KJV).

The third victim is the skeptic who stands by and condemns this act and the resulting loss as wicked or evil. Two things follow. The first is the contradiction that has already been established—that the one who makes such a condemnation has no basis for a moral law by which the condemnation is made. Certainly, mindless evolution that is "red in tooth and claw," to quote Tennyson, does not provide a moral basis for this philosophical castigation, does it? In fact, if we are indeed the random product of evolution then aggression and domination are in themselves good things, because at least they assure survival of the fittest. But in our moral frame of reference God reminds us that death and separation are graphic reminders in a hastened form of what inevitably awaits those who choose to live apart from God. To those people, evil and destruction are logical outworkings, whether in a slow measure or in a dramatic one.

Indeed, the rupture of relationships and death and pain are all present evils that we live through. But here a second important consideration challenges the skeptic. Evil must always be defined in terms of purpose. How can anything exist without first establishing purpose? Without purpose, destruction is a meaningless term. God's purpose for us is that we live for Him who is the very source of our being. Only in Him, the one who has planted love, mystery, and worship into our hearts, is purpose fulfilled. When we thwart that purpose, the greater evil is not death or suffering, for life can be restored. The greater evil is in choosing to separate ourselves from God and live contrary to His purpose.

It is for this reason that Dostoevsky defined hell as the inability to love. Hell is only the confirmation of a will that has chosen to deny Him His terms and to live apart from Him. C. S. Lewis said that there are two kinds of people in this world, those who are willing to bend their knee and say to Him, "Thy will be done," and those who refuse to bend their knee and He says to them, "All right, thy will be done."

Someone might counter, "But why do His terms give us only one way to Him?" The answer is that even had He given us a thousand and one ways, the skeptic would always want one more way because at the heart of evil is autonomy—self-law and self-love. Self-law will always lead to the loss of law and self-love to the loss of love. The skeptic's criticism of evil is logically and existentially self-defeating.

This brings us to the fourth "victim," the questioner who asks, "How is it that God could be sovereign over death but we do not individually have the same right to take a life?" Neither our character nor our capacity warrants such a self-arrogated authority over life's sanctity. God alone will always act in character, out of holiness, out of purity, and will never do that which is wrong. Human beings cannot take the same prerogative in acts that we call atrocities because we neither have the character to make the right choice nor the power to restore life.

God can allow such events to happen, for He alone can restore life through those tragedies and reveal the destructiveness of sin through tragedies, being perfect in His decisions, pure in His reason, and able to give strength to those who seek His comfort. We cannot claim such absoluteness. Our characters are not pure. Our decisions can easily be based on wrong information and wrong motives. Is this not the reason the law exists and powers are established in the land, so that each individual does not have the right to avenge every wrong? Even so, we see how states and governments can err with all the measures the law takes to protect the innocent.

These pitfalls and our proneness to error make it clear that the tragedies and atrocities we see ought to cause us to flee to God and to recognize how deceitful the human mind is. How desperately we are in need of wisdom and character or, as the Scripture writers put it, in need of a changed heart and an empowered will that we might live for Him.

Malcolm Muggeridge once wrote to Mother Teresa, saying that he had no interest in the church or in the Christian faith because of all the duplicity he had seen there. Mother Teresa, who spent her life surrounded by pain and misery, wrote back to him and said, "Your problem is a finite one. God is infinite. Let the infinite take care of your finite struggle."[2] Muggeridge bent His knee to Christ and called it the most fulfilling step he had ever taken in his life.

THE WORLD AS WE KNOW IT

Only one brief idea needs to be added. Is this, then, the best of all possible worlds God could have made? Very plainly put, to our way of thinking there are only four possible worlds that scholars have talked about. The first is that there be no creation versus this world. Would it not have been better for God to have created no world rather than to have created this one where good and evil are possibilities? The second is to have created a world where only good would have been chosen, a kind of robotic world. The third option would have been a world where there was no such thing as good or evil, an amoral world. The fourth is this world that we live in, where good and evil exist along with the possibility of choosing either.

As soon as we introduce the question of what would have been better we again invoke an absolute point of reference, and that we can only introduce if God exists. In the final analysis, of the four worlds described ours is the only one where love was genuinely possible. The love of a mother for her child. The love of a man for his wife. The love of a friend for a friend. The love of a man or a woman for God. We must recognize that love is the supreme ethic that we know of, and where love is possible, freedom and the possibility of suffering accompany it. In His character, God alone is the absolute expression of love that is never separated from holiness. God cannot be at the same time holy and unloving or loving and unholy. In turning our back upon Him, we lose the source of defining love, live with the pain of unholiness, and suffering remains an enigma—leaving our blemished characters in search of a moral law and our finite minds crying out for an answer. Which of us does not hurt when we see a pure love abused and despised? Our hearts reveal a hunger for a love that is pure, and in this world we have lost both definitions because we have denied their source.

When we come to Jesus Christ at the cross, where love, holiness, and suffering combine, we find both the answer to why we suffer and the strength to live in this mortal frame for Him. For here holiness and love were attacked in the name of political and religious fervor. Here suffering was poured out without measure, yet triumph awaited. As we come to the cross and from there live out our lives for Him, we make the extraordinary discovery that the cross and the resurrection go together. Where love is possible, there pain is also possible. Where the resurrection is promised, there is also the promise of tears wiped away. Heaven is the confirmation of our choice, to love Him and to be with Him. That is the hope of everyone who is a follower of Jesus Christ, whom to know is life eternal. Hell is the confirmation of spurning God's answer and hope and of living with the entailments of our ability to procreate but also to destroy without recovery.

To answer Ivan Karamazov's question, if I were perfect in goodness and had the power to create life and to restore it, I would not see the loss of life the way Ivan saw it. If, on the other hand, I had the power to create life without the moral purity to guard it or the strength to restore it, then I ought not to create that life. But the only reason I say "ought not," is because I know what should be deemed good and what should be branded wicked. That "ought not" comes to me from God, who does have the power to create and the power to restore, the sovereignty to take a life and to comfort us in our loss. He has asked us to trust in His power, His purpose, and His character.

Ivan's question is a warning to us not to play God. It cannot be an indictment against God for whom the same limitations of power and wisdom do not apply.

THE THEOLOGICAL IMPERATIVE

That is why God's great desire is that we see our hearts before Him as He does, recognizing that we are not qualified to make moral judgments apart from Him. Like Job, when we come to Him as Creator and Designer, Revealer and Comforter, Mediator and Savior, we find that He is also the Strengthener and Restorer. On the basis of what we know, we can trust His character for what we do not know. That may be why Mother Teresa's last utterance was four small words as she prepared to meet her Savior. Living in a city whose pain and suffering are proverbial, she found the only answer that was worthy of her being. Her last words were, "I love You, Jesus." She took His love to a city and a world in need. Every other answer to the problem of pain not only fails to satisfy, it fails to even justify the question.

Endnotes

Chapter 1. The Cry to Know God

1. Charles Haddon Spurgeon on Malachi 3:16, quoted in Arthur W. Pink, *The Attributes of God* (Grand Rapids, Mich.: Baker, 1975), 89.
2. This story is also shared in Rolando E. Villacorte, *The Real Hero of Edsa* (Quezon City, Philippines: Berligui Typographics, 1988), 135.
3. J. P. Moreland and Kai Nielsen, *Does God Exist? The Great Debate* (Nashville: Thomas Nelson, 1990).
4. Read R. C. Sproul, *The Psychology of Atheism* (Minneapolis: Bethany Fellowship, 1974).
5. A. W. Tozer, *The Knowledge of the Holy* (Lincoln, Neb.: Back to the Bible, 1971), 111.
6. Tozer, 62.
7. Used by permission.
8. William Blake, "The Tyger," in *Songs of Experience,* 1794.
9. This discussion is developed from F. W. Boreham, "The Candle and the Bird," in *Boulevards of Paradise* (London: The Epworth Press, 1944), 112.

10. Arthur Hugh Clough, "Say Not the Struggle Nought Availeth," quoted in Boreham, "The Candle and the Bird."

Chapter 2. The Cry to Feel My Faith

1. Daniel Goleman, *Emotional Intelligence* (New York: Bantam, 1995), 3.
2. David Gelertner, "How Hard Is Chess?" *Time,* 19 May 1997.
3. William Cowper, "Walking with God," in *A Choice of Cowper's Verse,* selected by Norman Nicholson (London: Faber & Faber, 1975), 23.
4. Goleman, 80.
5. Os Guinness, *God in the Dark* (Wheaton, Ill.: Crossway, 1996), 134.
6. William M. Runyan, "Lord, I Have Shut the Door."
7. Oswald Chambers, *My Utmost for His Highest* (New York: Dodd, Mead, 1935), May 20.
8. Martin Lloyd-Jones, *Spiritual Depression: Its Causes and Cure* (London: Pickering & Inglis, 1965), 21.
9. Katharina A. D. von Schlegel, "Be Still, My Soul," trans. Jane L. Borthwick.
10. Elie Wiesel, quoted in Dennis Ngien, "The God Who Suffers," *Christianity Today,* 3 February 1997.
11. Anne Taylor Fleming, "The Right Thing to Do," *Ladies' Home Journal,* July 1997.

Chapter 3. The Cry for a Reason in Suffering

1. David Hume, source unknown.
2. Source unknown.
3. Fyodor Dostoevsky, *The Brothers Karamazov,* trans. Andrew R. MacAndrew (New York: Bantam, 1981), 296.
4. Bertrand Russell, *Why I Am Not a Christian* (London: Unwin Books, 1967), 146.
5. Annie Johnston Flint, "He Giveth More Grace."

6. Malcolm Muggeridge, quoted in Donald McCullough, *Waking from the American Dream* (Downers Grove, Ill.: InterVarsity, 1988), 145.
7. G. K. Chesterton, "The Ethics of Elfland," in *Orthodoxy* (Garden City, N.Y.: Doubleday, 1959).
8. A lie that many have bought into is the Darwinian evolution theory. It has recently been articulated by a professor of biochemistry from Lehigh University. Michael Behe has powerfully demonstrated that meeting Darwin's own challenge of what it would take to falsify his theory comes from biochemistry. Behe's book, *Darwin's Black Box,* is a masterpiece. Richard Dawkins, the arch-Darwinist from Oxford, has angrily denounced Behe as "intellectually lazy" and adjured him to "go find an answer" to support the theory of evolution from within Behe's own discipline. One has to wonder where the lines of reason and unreason become blurred when intellectuals such as Dawkins defy the logic of scientific findings.
9. Read Michael Polanyi, *Personal Knowledge* (London: Routledge & Kegan Paul, 1962).
10. A friend of mine, a professor of chemistry, sent me this curious item to enjoy. His letter said, "In 18 milliliters of water (about two swallows) there are 6 x 10^{23} molecules of H_2O. How big is 10 to the power of 23? A good computer can carry out 10 million counts per second. It would take that computer two billion years to count 10 to the power of 23. If that is not awesome enough, look at it this way. A stack of five hundred sheets of paper is two to three inches high. How high would the stack be if it had 6 to the power of 23 sheets? That stack would reach from the earth to the sun, not once, but over one million times. That is the vastness and density God has put into this creation." He ended the letter by saying, "What an awesome God!"
11. Mike Otto, "Looking Through His Eyes."
12. William Cowper, "God Moves in a Mysterious Way."
12. Fanny J. Crosby, "All the Way My Savior Leads Me."

Chapter 4. The Cry of a Guilty Conscience

1. See Robert Karen, "Shame," *The Atlantic,* February 1992, 44–70.
2. William Shakespeare, *Macbeth,* act V, scene 1, line 28.
3. George Gordon Byron (Lord Byron), quoted in *The International Dictionary of Thoughts* (Chicago: J. G. Gerguson, 1969), 346.
4. Peter Malkin in *The Jerusalem Post International Edition,* 28 March 1992.
5. Benjamin Franklin, quoted in *The International Dictionary of Thoughts,* 583.
6. Alexander Pope, quoted in *The International Dictionary of Thoughts,* 584.
7. C. S. Lewis, quoted in *The International Dictionary of Thoughts,* 584.
8. Peter Kreeft, *For Heaven's Sake* (Nashville: Thomas Nelson, 1986), 98.
9. Saint Thomas Aquinas, the *Summa,* quoted by Peter Kreeft in *For Heaven's Sake,* 96.
10. From an interview with Richard Dortch in *Christianity Today,* 18 March 1988.
11. John Donne, in *The Oxford Book of English Verse, 1250–1900* (England: The Oxford University Press, 1924), #201.

Chapter 5. The Cry for Freedom in Pleasure

1. Malcolm Muggeridge, *Vintage Muggeridge: Religion and Society,* ed. Geoffrey Barlow (Grand Rapids, Mich.: Eerdmans, 1985), 21.
2. Neil Postman, *Amusing Ourselves to Death* (New York: Viking, 1985), vii.
3. Sigmund Freud, quoted by Heinrich Meng and Ernest Freud, eds., *Psychoanalysis and Faith: The Letters of Sigmund Freud and Oskar Pfister* (New York: Basic Books, 1963), 61.
4. F. W. Boreham, "Phoebe's Perplexity," in *Wisps of Wildfire* (London: Epworth, 1925), 79–80.
5. Frank B. Minirth and Paul D. Meier, *Happiness Is a Choice* (Grand Rapids, Mich.: Baker, 1994), 13.

6. Susannah Wesley, quoted in *Topical Encyclopedia of Living Quotations,* ed. Sherwood Eliot Wirt and Kersten Beckstrom (Minneapolis: Bethany House, 1982), 227.
7. Rich Wilkerson, *Private Pain* (Eugene, Oreg.: Harvest House, 1987), 123.
8. Minirth and Meier, 60.
9. Malcolm Muggeridge, *Jesus Rediscovered* (Garden City, N.Y.: Doubleday, 1969), 77–78.
10. Arthur Sullivan and Adelaide Proctor, "The Lost Chord."
11. G. K. Chesterton, *Orthodoxy* (Garden City, N.Y.: Doubleday, 1959), 160.
12. C. S. Lewis, *The Screwtape Letters* (Grand Rapids, Mich: Baker, 1969), 51.

Chapter 6. The Cry of a Lonely Heart

1. Thomas Wolfe, "God's Lonely Man," in *The Hills Beyond* (New York: Plume/New American Library, 1982), 146, 148.
2. D. H. Lawrence. Source unknown.
3. C. S. Lewis, *The Abolition of Man* (New York: Macmillan, 1947), 87.
4. C. S. Lewis, *The Four Loves* (New York: Harcourt Brace Jovanovich, 1960), 192.
5. Lewis Thomas, quoted in Paul Brand and Phillip Yancey, *Fearfully and Wonderfully Made* (Grand Rapids, Mich.: Zondervan, 1980), 25.
6. F. W. Boreham, "The Sword of Solomon," in *The Blue Flame* (London: Epworth, 1930), 29–30.
7. Sister Mary Rose, president of Covenant House, New York City, *Covenant House Newsletter,* Fall 1995. Used by permission.
8. Frederick Buechner, *The Longing for Home* (San Francisco: Harper Collins, 1996), 11.
9. Lewis, *The Four Loves,* 32–33.

Chapter 7. The Cry of God for His People

1. *The Christian Century,* 10 May 1961.
2. Charles Wesley, fourth verse of Samuel Wesley's hymn, "O Thou Who Camest from Above."
3. William McChesney, quoted by Joseph T. Bayly, *Martyred* (Grand Rapids, Mich.: Zondervan, 1966), 121.
4. There are many spurious expressions of all kinds of worship that reveal the desperate hunger for something spiritual. Certain forms of mysticism have become extremely popular because they induce people into a sense of worship. But when the philosophies undergirding those expressions are evaluated, there is a fragmentation at the core, and it will only be a matter of time before their bankruptcies are revealed. True worship can only be experienced when we worship the true and living God and do so in spirit and in truth.
5. William Temple, quoted by David Watson, *I Believe in Evangelism* (Grand Rapids, Mich.: Eerdmans, 1976), 157.

Postscript to Chapter 3, The Cry for a Reason in Suffering

1. C. S. Lewis, *The Problem of Pain* (New York: Macmillan, 1966), 26.
2. Malcolm Muggeridge, *Something Beautiful for God* (New York: Ballentine, 1971), 117.